I AM THE BEACON

An Extraordinary Journey of Awakening
in These Times of Ascension

SHAWNA L. FRANCES

Cosmic New Earth Publishing, USA
Library of Congress Control Number: 2020912153

Cover Design by 100Covers.com
Interior Design by FormattedBooks.com

I dedicate this book to my amazing dad. While he struggled with my awakening process, and still does to some degree, he loves me unconditionally and gives me unwavering support. This has made all the difference.

Contents

INTRODUCTION

For us as Players on the path to service to others, our stairway 'lies on the whispering wind' of spirit. Nothing is known. We are not in control. We dwell in mystery, paradox and unknowing. We have no material proof that our faith has merit, only intuition. We never shall have any such proof, except subjectively.

As we look back on our lives after being Players for a while, we will have much subjective proof that the whispering wind knows precisely what it is doing. At the beginning, though, we are all fools. We have only our faith as we step confidently into the abyss.

The whole point of faith is that we choose to take the leap into faith with no outer proof. We leap because we embrace the mystery, the paradox and the state of the unknowing which characterize a life lived in faith. We let these qualities call us forth into the mid-air of unproven faith. And we find our feet in that very mid-air, and come into our faith organically, once we make the leap.

- Living the Law of One 101: The Choice by Carla Rueckert

A MESSAGE FROM THE AUTHOR

When I stumbled into this journey the summer of 2018, I had no idea where it would take me. I'm having a hard time capturing in a few words what has transpired these past 18 months and how it has changed my life. What an incredible, extraordinary experience. One that continues to evolve for me in amazing ways.

Perhaps some of you who are reading this text picked it up on a whim. Maybe you have an awareness of the ascension and want to learn more. Possibly you are trying to make sense of unexplainable personal experiences. Whatever the reason, I'm glad you are here and I hope this book helps you with your own personal journey and unfolding.

What I'll say up front is that I don't want you to be scared. Not for me, or you, or for any reason. Fear is the antithesis of love. And love is what this is all about. What life's all about.

First, love for ourselves, then love for everything else. The embodiment of love helps us evolve as souls on this precious planet we call Earth.

I am still learning to live this way myself.

There are times I've felt my chest will burst open with the feeling of love. Gazing upon the faces of my newborn sons, seeing the sun slowly rise above the ocean, receiving a deep, nurturing hug from a loved one. We all have fleeting heart-bursting moments.

But it doesn't seem like many of us experience this love on a regular basis. Life can be pretty hard, right? Ours is a dense, isolating, challenging environment in which to be born and live. Especially in this moment in time.

These are particularly tough times for humanity.

Yet, also a time of transition and transformation on our planet, a time of ascension. A time for celebration.

Where we are all headed… is toward love.

Shawna L. Frances

A surprise calling:
CHANNEL A BOOK ON THE ASCENSION

When the energy flares, I pay attention. On October 2nd, 2018, I was awakened with a jolt of energy at 2:30 a.m. As I lay in bed waiting, completely still, I heard a sentence repeating in my head over and over: *"The dawn of a new era is upon us."* This was early in my awakening journey.

I jumped out of bed to capture this on my laptop. After I typed that first sentence, another came. And another. As the words flowed, I kept typing. After 90 minutes, the sentences stopped. I'd completed the first few pages of what would become a small, channeled book.

The early-morning wake-up calls and words continued for 18 straight days. I'd get up, type for an hour or so, go back to bed, get up to meditate and then start my day job. I'd print out what I had typed and read it over with curious wonder. To this day, I do not know the identity of this being who brought this information forward; an Ascended Master who wishes to remain anonymous.

I was pretty astonished by this process and more than a bit apprehensive. All that came through was way outside of my comfort zone in terms of the backstory on this ascension. If you read the book, you'll see that the ascension is bringing about some pretty harsh physical changes to Earth. I was told we're *"being readied for a major, literally earth-shaking transformation the likes of which have never been seen or recorded here on Earth before."* I was told that upcoming changes to Earth's magnetism will cause *"cataclysmic and seismic events that will topple mountains, create massive valleys and unearth that which has been hidden below Earth's surface."*[2]

I had a few direct conversations with my other-worldly, etheric support team about these scary concepts, as you'll see in this book. I asked tough questions and received pretty direct answers. Through my research and channelings, I do believe these destructive events will happen (in fact they're already happening) which will result in loss of human life (also already happening). All part of this ascension. It is all a necessary aspect of Earth transitioning to a higher vibrational state.

At a super high-level, the ascension involves three things. First, a cataclysmic show of force as our planet aligns to a higher vibrational frequency. Next, a raising of energetic vibrational frequencies for humans who live here now and those who will be born before this process has completed. And thirdly, a massive unveiling of consciousness, which will reveal the reality of who we are and the truth about ALL LIFE throughout all of creation.

The book I channeled provides a solid introduction to the ascension: what it is, why it's happening and how we can experience it. It presents a high-level overview of how we got here and how non-human negative energies and evil helped to create this world in which we live. We are being called to shun fear and hatred and start living lives from our hearts, from a place of love. The call to action for us is to choose love, not fear. This first short book is another clarion call for all those who resonate with the messages. To see we are in fact all ONE, made from the same stuff, doing the best we can as we learn our lessons and evolve as souls.

On the 18th day of these early morning channeling sessions, the sentences stopped. The Ascended Master told me that the book was complete and that I should publish it. Holy shit. Okay.

So many emotions—I was so humbled and honored to be serving in this way. Yet scared to put this material out there, knowing darn well I was not qualified to talk about this stuff. This subject matter (and the method in which it was revealed) are just too unbelievable for most people. I was scared I may have gotten the messages wrong or hadn't channeled it clearly. Scared of what people would think of me, especially my friends and family who've known me forever.

But I felt the urgency to get the book out there to the public.

I had a $100 cover designed and published it on Amazon Kindle. The title was also provided by the Ascended Master: *Archangels, Aliens and Prophecies: The Cosmic Unveiling of a New Earth*.

At this point, I shared a few of my key experiences with my family and a couple close friends. It was really tough for them to grasp. My husband, dad, and my best friend all had their own reactions, none very supportive at first. Lots of fear, sadness, and anxiety. What's happening? Where is all this coming from? Are you talking to aliens? Angels? What is Shawna becoming? Has she lost her mind?

Funny thing, my life was about to get a whole lot crazier. I'd only scratched the surface.

More channeling: JOHN THE BAPTIST

What the hell does John the Baptist have to do with my awakening? Well, I'm not 100% sure. Here is what happened. As soon as the *Archangels, Aliens and Prophecies* book was complete, that same night in fact, I was "told" that I was to write another book. During this time I was frequently interacting with an archangel by the name of Archangel Metatron. Metatron delivered this message to me in grand fashion.

It was 11:43 p.m. on October 20, 2018. Lights were out and I was drifting to sleep. Suddenly, my body began vibrating in a way unfamiliar to me. And as I've said before, when the energy flares up, I pay attention. I laid there freaking out a bit. A message entered my mind that this new book would be a large book, epic in nature, very different from my first short, channeled book. It'd require intense focus and a lot of my time. Metatron said that this would be *John – The Soul Book*. He said, "Ascended Master John." I wasn't sure to whom he was referring.

He indicated this would be a continuation of another book, and I wasn't sure what that meant, either. He told me I'd start that night.

For almost three hours early into the morning, after midnight, he began pumping me full of what I'd call cosmic energy. Waves of bliss building and receding, raising my vibration. I saw flashes of light. It was beautiful. I was awakened at 6 a.m. with a jolt of energy.

Time to get started on this new assignment.

About this book: I AM THE BEACON

This book you are reading now started out as my type-written journal of what I thought would be *John – The Soul Book*. It starts on October 23rd, 2018, a little over a year ago at the time of this writing.

Although it didn't turn out to be a new epic tale about John the Baptist, it became my detailed journal of the past year of my awakening journey. And what a year it has been! I am so grateful and humbled by this very hard and so very extraordinary time. I'm still coming to grips with what is happening to me and how it's changing my life. I am still coming to terms with my mission.

Every word is the truth, my truth. I've fabricated NOTHING. I include transcripts from dozens of channelings and conversations with my other-worldly support team. Four hand-written journals are filled with my experiences in addition to what's presented here, captured and channeled. Nearly 100 of my personal dialogues and channelings are currently captured in my hand-written journals or recorded on my phone. This book includes only a handful.

My higher self and support team are urging me to publish my journal as a book. Well shit, again. Okay!

Since all this craziness started last summer, I stopped drinking alcohol, became a vegan and now I'm a vegetarian. I lost 35 pounds. I quit my high-paying job as a digital marketing vendor for Nike. I moved, by myself, to a small town in Mexico on the Baja peninsula to help raise my vibration. I began an etheric relationship with my twin flame who is not of Earth. While in meditation, traveling in my Merkaba, I've experienced incredible revelations. More incredible conversations have transpired with my angelic and galactic support team. I experienced such beauty and bliss in Mexico, feeling more comfortable in my skin than I've ever felt. All of this is captured in this book.

I've come to know my mission in life and I am whole-heartedly on my journey to fulfill it. I've begun to learn about the true multi-dimensionality of life, felt the presence of a greater power and have been fortunate to experience immense love pouring in from galactic and angelic realms. My heart is opening and I'm experiencing life in a new way. I'm starting to understand what it means to be one with everything and to share that love whenever and wherever I can.

I am transforming. I am transitioning. I am mourning for the loss of my old life while celebrating the birth of the new. I'm questioning everything—not only who and what I am, but what ALL of this is—every bit of it. And it's more amazing that my tiny little human mind can even begin to comprehend. Thank you for taking this journey with me. I am so honored to be of service.

I am the beacon for those who seek it.
I am the strength for those who need it.
I surrender in faith and in love.

About me: MY BACKGROUND

I grew up in a loving middle-class family with a younger brother and sister. My dad worked in sales for a major railroad most of his life. As he moved up the corporate ladder, we moved from city to city until I reached high school. My mom held several jobs selling real estate, working the phones at a suicide hotline and helping mentally challenged and handicapped adults with basic living skills. Always into New Age spirituality, she is how I gained my appreciation for the esoteric. We never attended church, and I grew up pretty ignorant about the major stories of the Bible.

Mom was very good at Tarot, owning both the Aleister Crowley Thoth tarot deck and *The Tarot Handbook* by Angeles Arrien. Consulting the Tarot, we'd often find useful and insightful guidance together. She was also an acrylics and watercolor artist, a free-thinker and, in her daughter's humble opinion, an authentic hippy. She loved nature and had a huge soft spot in her heart for all creatures great and small, from spiders and lizards to cats and cows. She was an immense nurturer, particularly for the underdog, the down-trodden and the disenfranchised. At one point, she worked in respite care for the Department of Health and Human Services, caring for foster kids who had attempted suicide. Kids came straight from the hospital into my mom's loving and safe home where they rested and escaped whatever situation they were in, at least for a short time.

Very dedicated to the railroad, my dad was successful at his job. He taught me the value of hard work, focus and tenacity. Just as he held a high standard for himself, I lived my own life with high standards, achieving my goals and working hard.

I always felt that my needs were met, and we always had plenty of love. But my parent's stress over money was also a stressor for me. They often used credit cards to make ends meet. I vowed that when I got older, I would have a successful, stable job and make good money at it. I'd have a nice house and a nice car and that would equal success and happiness.

As a Capricorn, I'm intelligent, practical, creative and driven. I'm self-reliant and stoic. I get things done. I'm ambitious. I'm also first-born which I believe amplified all these characteristics.

From an early age, I worked hard for good grades, had a few close friends and dabbled in school sports. I played the clarinet and alto saxophone, had a big social life and partied quite a bit in high school. I always had a steady boyfriend, though managed to keep my grades high and do well in school. As mentioned, I had my sights set on college and a high-paying career.

When I was 15, I got my first job at a fast food restaurant and developed a crush on a cute co-worker. We soon started dating and quickly became serious. Ten days after my 19th birthday, I gave birth to our first son, the light of our lives. What a beautiful gift, because I never wished to have kids. I thank my mom for her unconditional love and support for helping bring this precious little one into the world. I enrolled in college when my son was just six months old and worked part-time. After six years together, my boyfriend and I got married and had another beautiful son. Shortly thereafter, I received my Bachelor of Science degree in Organizational Communications.

Life back then was an amazing, busy whirlwind of chaos. Always so much going on with two active boys and a full-time job in digital marketing. My husband was a manager at a landscaping company and coached the boys' soccer teams. We shared a lot of time and memories with our close families.

When I was in my late teens, my aunt introduced me to energy work. Years later I became a Reiki Master. Discovering and feeling energy first-hand was life-changing for me. For the past 15 years, I've experienced bursts of sensual, blissful energy waves that course through my body. I've come to call them "energy blasts." Sometimes, they are so strong that they leave me breathless and in an altered state of consciousness. They can last anywhere from 15 seconds to an hour and leave me scratching my head…wondering what is this…and why am I experiencing it? My energy blasts have also anchored me into my knowingness of how profound and powerful energy can be.

Reading up on quantum physics, I learned how everything is energy—from solid objects to our bodies and even to the thoughts we have in our heads.

In my studies, I've also participated in a few psychic classes and trainings in hypnosis and past-life regression. I came across a mind-boggling book on craniosacral healing, *The Heart of Listening* by Hugh Milne which introduced me to a whole new world of energetic healing through visionary craniosacral manipulation. I was blown away by the teachings and concepts which touched on how our bodies, minds, spirits, energies all work together to form and also heal disease, emotional issues and ailments. I took craniosacral healing courses in California and enrolled in massage school in Portland, Oregon. As I attended massage school at night, I worked full-time by day in a high-stress job and helped raise our family. As my career advanced, I eventually chose not to pursue an alternative healing practice and instead focused on my digital marketing career. While digital marketing has a creative side, it required extreme focus, left-brained critical thinking, serious data analysis, and sound judgment in a fast-paced, highly competitive environment that included tight deadlines and little support. I exceled at developing trustful and friendly relationships with my clients, part of my career I enjoyed the most.

During this go-getter time, I kept a tiny bit connected to my spiritual side by reading *A Course in Miracles* by Helen Schucman and Neale Donald Walsch's *Conversations with God* series, the first mainstream channeled materials I ever read. I describe channeling simply as a human being bringing forth information from the spiritual realm. I find the backstories on most authors who publish channeled material fascinating. *A Course in Miracles* is a massive body of work that Helen Schucman worked on with her partner, William Thetford, from 1965 to 1972. Helen and William were Professors of Medical Psychology at Columbia University's College of Physicians and Surgeons in New York City. She described herself as atheistic and non-spiritual person, focused mainly on her career and status at a prestigious institution. Their work environment had become contentious and strained, at which point William declared, "There must be a better way."[3]

At that moment, Helen began to see strange images and have symbolic dreams, which she documented. Three months later, she received what she termed The Voice which seemed to give her rapid inner dictation. She surprised herself early on by writing, "This is a course in miracles." As quick as The Voice spoke, Helen wrote out in shorthand what was dictated to her in a notebook. At first this process made her very uncomfortable, but it didn't occur to her to stop. She attributed this inner voice to Jesus and came to realize that she had a special assignment along with her partner William.

William typed out all her notes each day as she read them aloud. She said that she would not have been able to complete the work without William's effort and support.[3]

Before he started writing the *Conversations with God* books, Neale Donald Walsch had careers in radio, marketing and newspaper editing. A series of unfortunate life events, including a fire that destroyed all his belongings, a divorce and an accident which broke his neck, the course of his life was changed forever. He lost everything and found himself living homeless in a tent in a park.[4] In anger, he wrote to God demanding answers. At the end of his letter, the pen he was holding began to move on its own—pouring out words and ideas to the page. Completely shocked, he didn't stop and went with it. His hand-written dialogue with a voice he attributes to God lasted for three years before he published the first book.[5]

Dictation from Jesus? Conversations with God? C'mon, right? Don't knock it till you try it.

I believe that transmissions, channelings, dialogues, discourses and information coming from other-worldly sources come through each channeler's personal set of filters which will undoubtedly influence the material on some level, even if it is just in the selection of words. Some people are "trance channelers" who become unconscious and are in a trance during transmissions and do not remember a thing. Perhaps this material is less tainted by their own influence, but I don't know. I am no expert in channeling and all the different ways channeling has happened in the past. I only know how it's happened for me. I say use your own discernment with any channeled material. If it resonates with you, great. If not, leave it behind.

There are so many sources of channeled material, from all kinds of beings and collectives from all matter of dimensions, star systems and etheric realms. There will be different levels of clarity and accuracy of these transmissions. If something touches your heart, or flares up your energy, or even leaves you confused or angry, possibly there is something there for you to consider.

My own recent experiences with channeling have blown the door wide open for me in terms of my belief in and acceptance of this form of powerful communication and support coming in from different realms. We are not alone in the universe, not by a long shot!

MY RECENT "AWAKENING"

In June, 2018, I came across a psychic's old business card in my desk and I felt a strong urge to visit. This medium introduced me to my spirit guide Micah. I discovered we are on our 20th life together, and I was able to have a bit of a dialogue with my spirit guide for the first time.

I was so excited! The next day, I chose to focus on creating a conscious connection with Micah through meditation. I began to journal his words in real-time, like automatic writing. I'd write my questions and thoughts. When Micah had an answer or response, I'd hear his words in my mind and write them down as fast as I could.

Through this exchange, I developed my telepathic listening skills and began to understand what it meant to channel. This was very powerful for me. I had always journaled and gotten general messages that I felt were supportive, but this was my first time really hearing that voice and understanding that something larger than my intuition was at play.

A few days into our dialogue, Micah verbally got my attention and sent an energy blast so deep it knocked me off my feet! He told me this was my gift and I would be sharing it with others. He told me to call upon other entities to help with this type of healing. This healing would involve deep core energy work. It was an epiphany moment. OMG, were my energy blasts somehow related to my spirit guide? Had Micah been doing this all along? I asked him.

I didn't get a very straight answer from him. He said it was complicated and did his best to explain it through words and images. I began to feel like I was understanding this energy more and more… and I knew that maybe I wasn't going crazy.

Every few days, he'd send in that energy and I'd receive so much love and bliss.

It was awesome and I developed a very special relationship with Micah in a short amount of time. My spirit guide helped me to understand that I'd be entering a major life transition and that the universe was very excited for me to enter this new phase. He also communicated that the planet's vibration was "speeding up" and I'd be helping with this. I was perplexed. I had no idea what he was talking about.

The next month, my amazing, loving mom passed away after a long fight with COPD, a lung disease that affected her breathing. I considered my mom to be my best friend. What a beautiful, heart-touching experience to be with her by her side as she passed. Really ready to go, she was fully at peace with her decision. We were both fully supported by God, Micah, and by many angels—the loving oversight was palpable.

The next day, Micah told me to find an energy healer who could help me with the grief. About three weeks later, Micah left me as well. He transitioned away and I was completely devastated. I cried for hours as I felt a part of my soul was being torn away. It was so surprising how deeply it felt, almost as hard as my own mother's passing. Although I had no idea this could happen, online research showed me that it happens quite a bit.

As Micah exited, two new spirit guides came in: Ruby and Rufus. Ruby offered comforting, assuring words, while Rufus became my energy guide. Rufus was very different than Micah, not as talkative, but the energy was amazing. He provided those same sensual energy blasts Micah had sent for all those years. I was feeling better with each passing day.

The following month, I found an energy healer as Micah had recommended; a Reiki master who did something called "Metatronian" therapy. I had never heard the word before, had no clue what it meant, but my energy went crazy when I came across his bio. I was intrigued. I met with the healer and learned about Metatron, an Archangel of immense power who oversees other angels. As I did more online research, I came across the book *Metatron – This is the Clarion Call: All You Need to Know* which was channeled Robbie Mackenzie. Everything in my world completely changed as soon as I started reading this book. I refer to September 1st, 2018 as the beginning of my "awakening," the day I started reading this book. Explained simply, I was awakening to the true nature of existence. Wow!

The written words on the pages of that book sounded a bit crazy, but as I read along, blissful all-consuming energy occurred. My body was swimming in euphoric energy waves. The physical feelings were undeniable and unshakable, like I was coming home to an understanding that I'd never had before. I learned about the current ascension of humanity and Earth, concepts that were new to me. The book explored extraterrestrial support and Galactic hierarchies. It explained the urgency of following a life filled with love and non-judgment and the importance for each of us to step into our divine missions.[6] I couldn't put the book down.

I continued to marvel at the energy emanating from the book's extraordinary messages. Within a week, I began to hear Archangel Metatron's voice during my meditations and journaling. I was so humbled and honored. Soon, I was having regular conversations with him as well as his team who performed lots of energy work on me and pushed me to exercise, quit drinking, to only eat a plant-based diet. At that point, I began meditating for a couple hours a day. Metatron told me that I am critical to the awakening of humankind and that I am evolving quickly and beautifully.

This book also introduced me to the concept of the Merkaba, also known as Metatron's cube, a geometric figure made of two intersecting tetrahedrons, one facing up and one facing down, which spin in opposite directions. Envisioning yourself in the middle of this spinning cube while in meditation, the Merkaba is a gateway to other dimensions and gets you in touch with your higher self. Once you activate your Merkaba, your consciousness can visit any place in the universe at any time—past, present or future.[6] I started taking my own trips in my spinning Merkaba and found it completely fascinating.

Metatron introduced me to the concept of a twin flame. He told me that I'd be meeting mine soon and that our union would be critical for my mission. I learned many people are coming together with their twin flames at this particular time in order to help raise humanity's vibration here on Earth. The twin flame energies will be a major catalyst for the ascension of humankind.

This five-week roller coaster of biblical proportions caused me to struggle with all these messages and teachings. My soul believed these things, but my mind still resisted. Was I making all this up? Going crazy? What the hell was going on? I began to do more research on the ascension. Even a year later I'm still learning what this all means.

Three more channeled books by Robbie Mackenzie followed the *Clarion Call* book—an additional one from Metatron called *The Healing Book* and two books from the Galactic Council, a collective of highly evolved beings, not of Earth, who are providing support and oversight to us humans who are currently undergoing this ascension. Each book in the series provided unimaginable energy frequencies and mind-blowing material on what is going on here on Earth right now.

I offer to you, dear reader, the transmissions that have come to me and through me to be shared in this time in this place, as we all ascend to a higher vibrational frequency and way of living on Earth, together, moving toward love.

Please reach out and let me know how these channeled teachings resonate with you and where you are on your own journey and awakening. I am forever both humbled and honored to be bringing these words of wisdom to you and would love to hear from you.

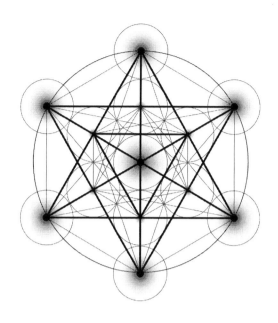

PART ONE:
GO WITH THE FLOW

Be not content with future happiness. It has no meaning and is not your just reward. For you have cause for freedom now.

- A Course in Miracles

(As I sat down to start this new "John - The Soul Book" in earnest, I was surprised when Archangel Metatron came through first with this foreword. I channeled these words two days before my first John the Baptist journal entry, which begins after this foreword.)

FOREWORD
BY ARCHANGEL METATRON

My beloved dear ones, it is such a pleasure and an honor to be communicating with you today. There is so much to tell you about, so much inspiration to provide. So much to communicate with you, particularly those who are feeling drawn to this book. There's a reason why you have picked this book up to read; you are ready for these messages. We Archangels and Ascended Masters are here to serve all of you in this mission. We want nothing but the best for all of you – to live your lives fully, and with love, on a clear path to ascension. This channel here has graciously provided herself, has given her free will, to channel these messages from myself and Master Ascended John the Baptist. We thank her so much for her service. She has been on quite the rollercoaster ride these past couple of months and is doing beautifully. We are here to support her with all of our love and light, just as we are here to support you with the same.

Keep your ears open. Take heed. Feel our presence. You are not alone, though it may feel isolating, you are surrounded by light, by love; surrounded by evolved beings who are doing nothing but focusing on the ascension of humanity right now. This is such an important and amazing time for all of you, unprecedented in Earth's history. Now is the time to heed the call, act on your inspiration. Grow into beautiful bright beings of light and shine throughout the galaxy. Never before in your lifetime and never again in your lifetime with this call be stronger, will this need be greater. It'll take each and every one of you to ascend past your earthly desires, beyond your root chakra, beyond your lower selves to help this process unfold as it needs to. This is the time my friends. Commit yourselves to this process, open yourselves to our messages. We invite you, if you are feeling so inclined, to become our mouthpieces here on Earth. We Ascended Masters and Archangels and evolved beings need as many volunteers as possible to help spread the word of love, to help eradicate negative forces and negative energy on the earth plane. It's such a critical time my friends, not for the faint of heart. You must decide, do you look forward with fearlessness and strength? Or do you look backwards, drop your eyes, bow your head and decide to be blind as to what is happening?

I know these words sound harsh. I am Metatron, after all. This is how I operate. But the directness here is full of love and compassion for each and every one of you. Everyone is deserving of this connection. Everyone is deserving of this light. Everyone is in fact made of this light; you just may have just forgotten that in this incarnation on Earth. We are here to help remind you, to help set you on the right path, and give you a gentle nudge forward so that you may walk brilliantly, standing tall, one foot in front of the other, purposefully into your missions. We all thank you from the bottom of our hearts for reading this book and taking action. With all the love of God Presence, with all the light I can muster, I bestow this upon you now.

October 23, 2018

John (as in John the Baptist) and I meditated together, he in front of me facing me. Me bringing him closer then pushing him back as I got my bearings. Acclimating to his presence. This is all so new, yet so familiar, so very exciting. What if this is real?

We sit and breathe for a few moments only, and then I feel him around my back, voice to my neck, arms encircling me, hands on my abdomen, my sacral chakra. This is how we'll communicate, he tells me. His voice coming from behind, the base of my skull, behind my throat chakra. It'll be gentle, sweet, casual, loving. I know his voice. I know that feeling, that sense of being seen, nurtured, held. I have yearned for this for lifetimes. I will never yearn for it again in this lifetime now that John has re-introduced himself. He's said so himself. So sweet.

He shows me some history, some visions. We walk the streets of an open-air town, he says it is Jerusalem. We walk up a stone spiral open-air staircase, up about 2 stories, and look over the city. I see a large town square, taller domed buildings in the distance, a river behind me. People and business below. Hot and dry and sunny. Dusty. Dust in my throat.

We walk down the spiral stairs and back onto the street. Let's walk he says. We slowly walk down the narrow walkway and I begin to lose my connection to this scene in my imagination. He brings me back by pulling me to him on the street, looking into my eyes. He begins to kiss me. That deep connection, that pleasure, that feeling of his lips on mine. I am feeling this deep in my heart. He tells me we are safe here. This is a shared creation of our own minds; we control what happens here. The people around us disappear and we have the entire town to ourselves. Empty streets, not a sound. I am safe here. He stops kissing me and begins to resume our walk. I stopped him and pulled him back to me, kissed him more, just in awe for this moment and what is happening, how I'm feeling. I start to cry, physical tears welling up in my eyes as I envision this moment.

We walk further down the alley way and there I see the brown boy with black hair from my vision with Jesus last week, Jesus' view for a new earth, playing and splashing in the water without a care in the world. When Jesus showed me this ideal new world last week, I saw this boy which represented the playful, child-like innocence in all of us. That which we must preserve and live every day. It represented how children were able to be children, to be themselves, to be in the moment and be who they are with complete enjoyment.

We walk further and I see an elderly woman praying. I see her face, her multi-colored cloth covering her head. She's elderly. She holds a rosary. I ask John, is this after the time of Jesus? She is holding a rosary, with a cross on it. Yes, this is the time of Jesus and he has not yet died on the cross, but the rosary here represents the idea that many people are praying to and worshipping Jesus.

These are the common people. These are members of the unseen masses. Those who lead simple lives, care for their families, take care of their basic needs. They are worshipping in secret. Gathering in groups of 3, 7 and beyond. The parallels with the Galactic Council book hit me squarely in my knowing. I am feeling this connection—the worshipping in secret, the surrender to Jesus, in secret, it is judged, it is misunderstood. Just like me today with my awakening, this new path I'm now walking. The meditations

3

we'll do is parallel to the praying that people did in Jerusalem at the time of Jesus' life. Those around me who don't understand and will judge me as crazy and selfish. I must continue on.

The evil forces that moved into Jerusalem were so great that Jesus had to come there, to that particular area of the world. So fallen, so deep into corruption. The handful of people who chose to follow Jesus felt the love, the hope, related to this person and his messages of love. They knew that in this life, their church, their leaders were not to be trusted, were not there to lead them, to support them, but instead to control them and instill fear in them. Here in Jesus they found their inner voice, recognized who they were at their core. So strong was this instinct to follow Jesus that they'd rather die than not embrace this being of hope, this beacon of light. That living under oppression and fear was like being dead already. They had not much to lose and so much to gain by following in his footsteps.

John and I walk further, and we found ourselves in an expansive, golden meadow. This is not Jerusalem; it is a sacred place from within me. A beautiful potpourri of white, yellow, peach and orange flowers begin to grow up all around us, filling the air with their sweet scent. So incredibly beautiful. John is sitting and I am laying my head in his lap. He's stroking my hair, smiling down at me. This is such an intoxicating place for me. So safe. Here he leans down and whispers in my ear. I can't hear him, it is silent. But I imagine that my soul knows exactly what he is saying.

He places a hand over each of my chakras, from my head down, and tells me he's going to help work on my energy. Soon he's moved and he's now between my legs, on his knees, and he's positioned to enter my naked body. He enters me and I feel his sweet loving energy, so sexy, so blissful, he is going in slowly, out slowly, each time moving that soft gentle energy up my body, through my chakra system, until filling my heart with white love and light. He tells me to know and remember how this feels, this is his energy signature. Know this. Remember this. Recognize this. It is so sweet and euphoric, not jolting or invasive. Large and expansive. All encompassing. I am drunk with this energy.

At some point I crawl into his open third eye, we are both in this open dark space, with lights shining only on us. We are doing acrobats, our bodies free, me twirling in the air as he holds my hands, my body perfectly vertical, spinning, he gives me a gentle push up and I float upwards and twist around to horizontal. Falling into his arms as he catches me deeply. Then up I go again, gracefully and expansively twisting, contorting in the air like an artist, expressing myself with my body in this weightless state. John facilitating with supportive catches and tosses.

Now it is John's turn to lay in my lap. I whisper sweet nothings in each of his ears. I don't know what I'm saying, but my soul knows. To my ears I am silent. I start to give him Reiki on his heart, tracing the Cho Ku Rei symbol over his heart, feeling my hands heat up and vibrate. Seeing light in his heart area under my hands as the exchange of loving energy takes place. After a few minutes I move my hands to the side of his head and give Reiki there for a moment, looking down at this masculine face and form, he is shirtless. I then find myself at his feet. I begin to wash his feet with a yellow natural sponge, first the left. Slowly, lovingly. After I've bathed his left foot with the warm water, I put the sponge down and massaged the ball of his foot, his heel, his toes. Same with the right side. Wash, then massage. At the end I hold my thumbs in the center of each foot just below the balls of his feet and press their gently. This brings both our energy systems into homeostasis with complete gentle flow and peace.

Sharon Sananda Kumara, my incredibly gifted psychic friend who helped connect John and me last night, said that he and I would be bringing forward our story, our story of us. We've had many lifetimes together, even before the time of Jesus. John was already ascended when he embodied John the Baptist during Jesus' time. He had worked with Jesus in a previous life where he guided Jesus toward his mastery, reincarnating together so that John could continue to help Jesus with his ascension.

Possibly these notes are exactly how this story will unfold. Time spent with John in deep meditation, our shared visions, these visions that completely effect my physical, mental and emotional body as I sit here in the lotus position, in my living room, before the sun has even come up.

I am so honored and I feel so blessed to be part of this…what is "this"? I can't overthink it. Within a few weeks I'll know so much more. Remember so much more. Remember who I am fully.

October 24, 2018

Meditated with John for a few minutes and he guided me on some deep breathing from my diaphragm. He asked me to make my third eye as big as a window. I expanded it to a window, and I looked out the window to see soft rolling hills of yellow grass, with a pinkish gray sunrise happening in the distance. We stepped out of the window together and walked hand in hand into this scene. After a few steps John stopped and kissed me lightly on the lips for a few moments. He said we were safe here, this is a construct of our own minds, our souls, and we are in complete control.

I feel my mind wandering, thinking of other things, a song popping into my head. I have to get centered again, connect to Mother Earth, connect to the Christ grid. Breathe slowly and deep.

We walk a bit further and I notice I am barefoot in dark soil. Looking around we are now in a forest. An old forest, dense with trees and dark. We feel our bare feet in the ground, wiggle our toes. We are safe here. We climb over a big fallen tree and wait quietly. Then I notice there's a large area under this big tree, a camp has been dug out. A small area for a fire is under there, it's secluded. John and I sit facing each other and go into meditation. Soon we are joined by Jesus. This makes three. The three of us meditate together, cross-legged, making a triangle. Our heart chakras join in the middle with a gentle flowing buzzing power, and this energy shoots straight up into the heavens like a white column of smoke. This smoke encircles the globe.

Again, I feel my mind start to wander. I am losing the connection. I am thinking of other things. I am feeling so tired. What is wrong with me? I'm meditating with John the Baptist and Jesus and I can't keep present?

I'm no longer hearing John nor can I see him. I am so very tired. I take a sip of water and lay down on my couch, pulling a blanket up around me. I just need to sleep; I am sorry John.

In my dreams for the next 40 minutes, I am in a house that my family and I have moved into recently. It's built in the 70s and is a cool-looking house, but it's a mess, stuff everywhere. I ask my husband, why are we living here? Why are we maintaining two houses? He gets out a piece of paper to write out the expenses for both houses—our house that we currently live in and this new house. I am pleading with him, just tell me why we have two houses? What are we doing?

Then my son brings me a baby. This is my baby, but I forgot that I have him. I barely remember him, I've been so disconnected. He's hungry, but I can't remember if he can eat solids yet or what he even likes to eat. I'm so distraught. I feed him some bread and bacon. He's not happy with that. There are spiders and mice and clutter all about. I am so confused. We need to figure out which house we are going to keep. I have to focus on the children.

October 25, 2018

Oh my god. Such bliss with John. It's still hard to imagine this is all true. I question my worthiness. But I feel him so strongly. I see him. I hear him. Again, it is undeniable. The visions captured the past two days were outrageous, amazing. His sexual energy fills me so completely and deeply. Expansive and sparkling. It does feel like true core love. I am so blessed.

During meditation today John told me that soon I'd remember everything about myself. Everything about who I am. He'd open each of those doors with me.

As I meditated, I saw a man with a bald head lying on a massage table, naked. This startled me a bit. Then the man turned into John. Jesus suddenly appears next to me, to help me understand what I need to do for this healing. I placed my right hand at John's sacral chakra, left hand on his heart. I "boiled" the energy under my right hand, seeing clear energy bubbles churning up, feeling the gurgling, but no heat. I moved this boiling energy up his body, to his heart. I got to the throat chakra and used my right hand and intention to purge out the negative energy. I looked down and it wasn't John anymore, but the original man who was bald. He starts spewing and hissing out of his mouth as the energy rushes out of his throat chakra. His eyes are closed tight, face pinched, as if he is in anguish and pain.

October 26, 2018

With John and me, John explains we are truly one. One shared consciousness. All of this will be filtered through my higher consciousness. My higher self. In essence, I am creating this reality. There is no other way to do it, this is my reality. This is coming through my filter. It is the only way that I am able to imagine it, embody it, experience it, see it, is through my higher self. So yes, while John and I were in physical embodiment together over several lifetimes on this earth, he'll do his best to provide a perspective based on that individualized version of himself. But this does all come through my higher consciousness.

This will be of my creation. We're constantly creating our own realities, and this is no different, John explains. This consciousness that I'm in right now, there is only this one moment. Everything else as we go deep into the past will be constructs, things that we create, things that I create through my higher consciousness. But we have a shared consciousness, so this actually gets us closer to what we'd consider to be "facts" of what actually happened. During those embodiments there are things that happened, but they are through our filters because we create our own realities. But they are closer to fact than what you might otherwise imagine because of the shared consciousness. We are coming from one source.

Take a tree, for example. The tree is a carbon expression of the energy of *all there is*. Once that tree, that carbon, has lived out its life, it absorbs back into the earth, back into the energy field. The energy never goes away. The physical embodiment goes, but the energy stays and blends back into *all there is* to be individuated as another tree or another element of physical embodiment somewhere else, in another way and another form. We are doing the same thing. This is an expression of the divine. This is not *Shawna's experience*.

I decided to ask John if he wanted to come through with me channeling him. Here is what he said. (As I heard these words in my head, I said them out loud and recorded them on my phone.)

> "As John I'm actually a man of very few words. May be hard to believe because I did preach. But mostly I had inner dialogue happening, very much inward, connected to Source. Getting my guidance from source. Connecting to God. Most of my time spent listening to that voice and understanding it.
>
> "So that when I walked the earth and talked to people, my words were very selective. I had very specific things I was saying so that the message was crystal clear, and others could relate to it. The pure message of God, these messages of God are succinct, they're simple. So, I tried to live that every day. Mostly inward. Mostly listening. Mostly connected to source. Meditation was very important to me. As it should be for you, and as it has become for you.
>
> "I'm not really verbose. I will not be dictating to you pages and pages and pages of written testimony. I prefer to share with you in relationship, to impart those feelings that we have for each other, to help you raise your vibration and tap into this bliss. To help you along spiritually. All the while, helping you remember who you are.

"Our shared stories are going to emerge and yes, you'll write them down, but I will not be dictating. For what you and I have, this resonance and this vibration, speaks volumes in and of itself. Shawna, this connection is to your soul. You have to trust it. Draw upon it, embody it every day. Continue to see me clearly, understand what I'm saying without words. See our shared stories through pictures, imagery, shared experiences. You'll walk with me; I'll walk with you. We will float through this shared history together and these puzzle pieces will come together for you. This is why I'm here, Shawna, to help you remember who you really are. The veil will be non-existent."

Thank you, John. I am so humbled and blessed, and so appreciating you. I love you. *"And I you,"* he said.

October 27, 2018

This morning after my regular meditations, I said a prayer to connect to John—to be open, clear, available. Surrendering myself to him.

Again, John is meditating with me, this time directly in front of me. He is still and beautiful. I begin to feel the masculinity of him, radiating from his chest to my open heart. As my femininity connects with that masculinity, I feel completely disarmed. I feel my head lowering as if a need to bow down and pray comes over me. I put my hands together and allow my head to drop. John gets up on his knees and is doing something above my body. I can't see what he's doing but I sense it is similar to a Reiki attunement where he's tracing sacred shapes above my head, calling on energies to enter my aura. I get the feeling that these symbols or shapes will help me see our shared stories more clearly.

He tipped my head up to him and looked in my eyes and told me I would never again be lonely because he is with me always. Tears fill my eyes before I even had time to mentally process that statement. I cried for several minutes letting the truth of this sink in. The idea of loneliness has been a pretty well-hidden yet persistent part of me. I also miss my mom. It's only been three months since she passed away, but it feels like three years.

I then see myself laying down on a wooden table in a dark and simple room, imagining that I'm back in a place like Jerusalem. I'm wearing simple robes. John is standing over me, looking down at my face. Then I see that Jesus is standing on the other side of me. They each place their hands on me, alternating their hands from my root chakra up to my head, where John gently caresses my forehead down into my hair. I am clutching something at my chest, but I can't see what that is. Some type of religious symbol? As I see myself laying on this table, I understand that I'm sick. Fever. Chills. My life force very low. Is it Cholera?

John and Jesus are working on this for me. Again, the vision of "boiling" the energy. I see John's right hand over my lower abdomen and the energy below his hand is boiling—I see bubbles and churning and hear the sound of it. They bring this boiling up through each of their hands that rest just over my body. Soon all areas where their hands are hovering are boiling underneath. I come to understand that Jesus and John did many healings like this together, silently, without an audience. Again, the triad—Jesus, John, and me, their patient. The significance of working in threes coming up again. Possibly they are boiling and thus killing any bacteria, virus or harmful substance or energy causing my illness by working on the light body.

October 29, 2018

For a few days, my husband and I are in Mexico, on the Sea of Cortez. We're in a small town called Los Barriles, which translates to The Barrels, and checking out the surrounding area.

About 5 weeks ago, Archangel Metatron told me I'd be moving to the Sea of Cortez by myself to begin carrying out my life's mission. Now, I say this matter-of-factly, but at the time, this was such a wild, crazy, *impossible* idea. I am still working through this one mentally.

I understood this would be a temporary move to begin with, maybe six months.

The move would be happening around March 2019. Metatron told me that this was my higher self's plan for me. The work will be so intense and all-consuming that I'll need to be somewhat isolated, away from my current life, stepping fully into my new life. This would be a major turning point, with me quitting my job, leaving my family and venturing out on my own.

While living near the Sea of Cortez, I'll be raising my vibration level—my light, my capacity for embodying love energy—in order to help emancipate negative energy here on Earth. This is my life's mission, he tells me.

Metatron said that I'll be coming together and connecting fully with my twin flame's energy, and this will be the catalyst that powers up my vibration. He said I will learn everything I need to know to be able to emancipate negative energy.

So, we are here today, my husband showing all the support he can muster for this idea.

We are spending a few days checking out the town of Los Barriles, which gave me a strong energy pulse as I scanned the perimeter of the Sea of Cortez on a map trying to figure out whereabouts I should be heading.

Archangel Metatron told me that this place would provide me with the isolation I need, but also be abundant in things I love—swimming and snorkeling in crystal-clear turquoise ocean waters, sun, sun, sun, white sand, a nurturing environment for healing. I'd be meditating A LOT, traveling metaphysically A LOT, physically traveling when needed elsewhere, writing, teaching, channeling; very little eating. Swimming, sleeping, exercising. I'll be living very simply.

Today, Los Barriles was all about delightful "cuteness". We started our morning at 7 a.m. with a walk down the beach. With perfect timing, we came across a team of turtle conservationists helping 300 new little turtle hatchlings get into the ocean. Totally adorable, melt-your-heart cute!

We snorkeled right off the shore near our rented casita and first thing we saw a single puffer fish, skimming around on the sandy floor, picking at potential food. Completely cute.

My husband and I both are feeling in awe of Mother Nature today! So far, we are loving it here. Many times today I've felt gentle loving energy enter my chakras, just like little hugs.

My meditation with John the Baptist tonight was short but intense. I am seeing him here and there in random places, patient, serene, looking at me. Letting me know he's around. He's here in Los Barriles enjoying the scenery and relaxation with us.

I set my intention to connect and I felt him immediately.

He's in full lotus position in front of me. He is holding up two fingers together on his left hand and going back in forth with his hand between my third eye and his third eye. Back, forth, back, forth. This seemed to put me in the right space to connect quickly.

I go into his third eye. I land gently on the ground in a meadow full of what looks like wheat and yellow grasses. John is there, as he often is, on his side, chewing on the end of a golden wheat stalk. He's propped his head up on with his left hand, resting on his elbow.

I ask John if we were married in his lifetime as John the Baptist. He told me we were not married, but we were extremely close, like a soul mate but closer to a twin flame. We were not able to be married because it would be too dangerous for me. He told me we had a "secret, sacred relationship." The past few days I keep seeing a vision of him baptizing me in a river, and when he pulls me up out of the water, I look into his eyes and give him a deep and long kiss on the lips. This takes him by surprise. From there, I see us making love in a tent-like home, that flame between us burning so bright and wanting to burn higher, hotter. Unquenchable, almost destructive in its power.

He shows me the story of his death, whereby he was beheaded, to illustrate just how dangerous it would have been for me had we made our relationship public. I start to remember this. I start to remember how I felt when I heard that he had been beheaded. I was expecting him to come home any day, he was in a cell being held by the King. Any day they would release him. I had prayed and prayed for his release and felt it was imminent. A couple close friends broke the news to me that John had been killed in custody.

As I sit there meditating on this in my living room, my tears begin to flow. So strong is this memory, this imprint on me. While I was devastated at the time, I knew that we'd join together again someday. I had known even then of the vast and long-standing nature of our relationship.

I see Jesus next to me, arm around my shoulder, we are walking. He is so gentle, so loving. He is comforting me and talking softly of John and God's perfect plan. I am now back in the golden meadow with John, lying next to him as he's propped up on one elbow. He takes his other hand and places it on my heart. He tells me that I have a very special light within me that is impenetrable by dark energies. This makes my life here on Earth right now very special.

I have this heart of light that is particularly strong, and I am in human form on Earth which makes me somewhat of a secret weapon. Only I can do certain things here on Earth, things that those "on the other side" such as Archangels, Ascended Masters and other higher-dimensional beings are unable to do. John, Metatron, everything that is going on with me right now is all interconnected and part of a larger single plan.

I hear these words and my mind asks, why me? I certainly feel like an average, normal person, with not-so-loving thoughts, judgments upon others, anger at times. Fear for sure.

Is this my ego talking? Really puffing me up to be much bigger and more amazing than I am? Making me feel super special? What is really going on here?

I am just not sure. I guess a big part of me is just not believing it yet.

October 31, 2018

I am starting to see John more and more, usually he's casually watching me as I go about my day, and usually he's got the end of a strand of golden wheat in his mouth. I asked him why he's always chewing on a piece of wheat, and he said it was to make me feel more comfortable. It makes his presence seem more casual and aloof, versus him just watching me. Which it does.

Last night I was feeling some interesting and seemingly new energy fluctuations going on in my body. I had asked, "Who's there?" and went quiet for a moment. A bit later during a pretty intense meditation sequence and a few different channeling sessions, I was able to connect with John briefly. I see him again meditating in front of me. He tells me not to worry about where the energy is coming from or who is sending it. I just need to be open to receive it. Energy, love, support will continue to come to me from many sources.

Walking along the beach today in Los Barriles with my husband, we saw a dead and bloated eel, about 3 feet long. A dead puffer fish. A dead baby turtle at one of the marked nests. Several other dead fish and a couple fish heads with empty eye sockets. Tonight, on our way out to dinner, we also came upon a group of about 20 little new turtle hatchlings, just a foot or so from the receding surf. They were alive but very close to death. We are not sure what has happened with these little guys, why they either washed up to shore together in a group like that, or if they just couldn't quite make it to the water before they ran out of steam. We didn't know what to do. We carefully placed them in the water and watched the gentle waves take them out, little flippers coming to life in the water.

Metatron had told me two days ago that while the first part of our trip was about life, that we'd also experience death while here. Definitely that happened today.

Tonight, while meditating in our little casita, I asked if anyone in my support system had any insight regarding this trip to the Sea of Cortez to please communicate with me. What about the prospect of me moving here? Coming here by myself to carry out my divine mission? Metatron came through.

Metatron said that he can see that this had been a very special trip for me, full of beauty and grace, Mother Nature at her finest. His words that I recorded on my phone:

> "You're feeling connected to her so strongly right now. You've seen birth, and you've seen death. You've experienced bliss and love, such a deep connection with your husband… and even deeper with yourself. Being here is easy, right? You feel that easiness when you are here and how simple your life could be here.
>
> "The choice is still yours, and yours alone, and you have some time to ponder this. This path has been laid before you as an option, and I encourage you to consider it. This is not the only option, as you well know. And you are in choice in this matter.
>
> "Continue to feel into your heart. So much is going to change for you in the near future, and the few months between now and springtime. You will be a different person, Shawna. The person you are today, talking with me now, will be transformed within a few

short months. You'll have so much more wisdom and insight, and options available to you in your psyche, in your consciousness, all your levels of awareness.

"Your ability to manifest will be exponentially stronger. You'll be learning how to take advantage of all these gifts. As we've explained this is going to be a 100% full-time when you step into your mission. You'll need every bit of your focus on it at all times.

"You need to be in an environment where you are able to do that, cleanly, clearly. While also being able to take care of yourself. As we've mentioned, this area has strong nurturing quality, things that speak to your heart, things you value… sunshine, turquoise ocean water, nice people… It's a nurturing environment. We do think it would be very good for you. No decisions need to be made right now.

"Have faith. More than anything, have faith in yourself and your ability to make the right decision at the right time. Nothing will be done against your will. You will not be strong-armed into any decision here. We are co-creating. Your higher self has laid out a per-fect plan. And as the time comes to make these decisions, you will know the right decision and you will make it. Have faith."

Such a beautiful, loving presence. His words are equal parts terrifying and soothing. Continuing with my meditation, I reached out for John.

I picture John meditating in front of me, and I see me reaching out to gently touch his lips and cheek. He takes my hand and we get up and start walking. We are outside, we are smiling and giggling, walking hand-in hand through some tall golden grass into a treed area. We are excited. We reach a river. We are excited because we get to strip down naked and wash each other in this river. We quickly disrobe and walk into the water. I notice that my skin a rich brown color, including my nipples. My hair is also dark brown or black. We wade into the water, hand in hand.

John has his hands on my waist and he moves one of his hands between my legs to rest on my inner thigh. We both notice at the same time a few drops of blood running down my leg. Once I see the blood, I feel the cramping. And I feel horror wash over me. I know what is happening now.

From a detached place, I observe myself doubling over in pain. Soon my unborn baby, lifeless and only partially formed, moves out of me slowly. John is trying to help; I see the cord and other flesh in his bloody hands and the look of shock and fear on his face. The placenta follows, and we let it all fall into the river, floating downstream over small ripples of water. I continue to bleed heavily. I have just mis-carried our baby. The image of that fetus with the bloody attachments floating lifelessly down the river keeps playing in my head.

I come to know that this event preceded the bad fever I had which was healed by John and Jesus. My depression from the loss of our baby compromised my immune system so much that I, myself, had almost died.

November 4, 2018

We are home from the Sea of Cortez now. I haven't been completely without tears. Leaving the life I've known, what I've built… my identity… not without sadness. A part of me is completely excited, along with the parts of me that are uncertain, scared and sad. Metatron assures me that I'll know the right decision at the right time. Have faith.

Since coming back from our quick trip to Mexico, my connections with John have been a bit more fleeting. Yesterday after connecting, I saw myself being anointed and crowned. The room was quiet, lots of shadows, a sliver of sunlight coming in through one of the windows. I could see I was wearing a simple gown. The room seemed to be empty except for a couple onlookers. I could not see who was anointing me or placing the simple crown on my head. But in my mind's eye it seemed to be Jesus. I remember feeling very humble as this was happening to me.

This morning's meditation started with a few tears for my mom.

Going deeper into myself I state my intentions to connect with John clearly so that we can continue to explore our shared stories, our life together. I'm still feeling sad, so I do the Cho Ku Rei Reiki symbol over my heart and give myself Reiki. I then see Jesus place one hand on my forehead and one hand on the back of my head as he joins me in this self-healing. I start to feel a calmness come over me. I start to go deeper into my consciousness. He then has one hand on my heart and one hand continues to be at the back of my neck. Jesus tells me "Only love." I repeat that statement in my mind over and over. I feel this love opening my heart up. I feel myself feeling weightless, floating above my body. It feels so glorious, so effortless.

I know that I need to be coming from a place of love every day. Be in love every moment. I asked him to help me with this. Help me be in love every day. May I radiate that love always. I say a prayer asking for all people to be able to experience this love—to drop the illusions of fear and judgment, to support themselves, love themselves so therefore they can love and support others. I felt this prayer sound out from me with a feeling of massive spaciousness as if I was pronouncing it at a great hall.

After a few minutes, I reach out for John once again. I'd like to know how he preached to those who followed him during his John the Baptist lifetime.

I see myself sitting in a meadow with a couple dozen others, watching John speak. Though it doesn't look like John. This man is more slender, has shorter wavy hair that is more brown in color than the darker brownish black of John's hair. This man has more delicate facial features. I don't know who this person is, but he knows God and he is sincere.

As I sit here in my living room meditating, I feel the pull in my heart as this person spoke. I cannot hear the words, but I feel this love very intensely—and I see many hands of white energy reaching out from this person into each of the hearts of those who are sitting and listening. He has connected with each of our hearts so deeply. I feel this love, I see it shimmering around me and around the group. It is such an incredible feeling of nurturing, peaceful love. All is perfect with the world. Suffering forgotten.

This is the real message—the heart connection—not the words being spoken. But this shared divine love energy infused within each of us, coursing through our spirits. I feel this now as I type these words. So today is about the heart, opening to that energy, embracing and embodying this love. I still don't know who was speaking in that meadow, perhaps Peter? I understand now how the disciples and followers of Jesus back in those times would risk everything for this love, understanding and feeling. So powerful and beautiful. I want to walk in this space every day, every moment.

My vision ends with me burrowing my head into John's chest, we are laying down and I need him to hug me tight, to comfort me. Which of course he does. It feels so good to be seen and to be held like that.

Later that day I walked with the dog out to our yard and by the patio was a perfect single golden stalk of wheat, laying on the ground. I never see these around our house. I picked it up and felt a huge wave of sparkly energy flow from my head down to my toes. Thank you, John.

November 5, 2018

This morning, I did a standing meditation with John and Jesus, again the power of three. We combined our heart energies and intention for encircling the world with love into the center of us and shot it up to the Christ grid that surrounds the earth. Eventually this love energy encircled the entire planet. I felt drunk with this energy, literally head swimming, feeling light-headed, so peaceful yet radiant. It seems we're focused on Gaia (Earth) right now and all of humanity here. Healing intention.

I have started a 21-day cleanse today. Juice only for the next seven days, and mostly juice/water for the entire 21 days. I am praying for strength. Today is going well. The current book I'm reading, *Galactic Council Book 2*, channeled by Robbie Mackenzie, contains chakra downloads that were very intense this afternoon. So much energy movement, vibration, even my vision being affected as though I'm looking *through* things instead of *at* them.

Later this afternoon, feeling the need to meditate during a more intense energy episode, I see John in the doorway of my office. He's there to support me. I go into the living room to sit and meditate. I envision him holding me, cradling me really, my head supported on his chest, his arms around me. I feel like I'm being weak when we do this. Like I am not strong. I note that my ego doesn't like this. But my soul loves it. I see myself turn into a child in his arms—he's nurturing my inner child. I get up to finish my work.

November 6, 2019

The enlightenment of the 12. The enlightenment of the 12. The enlightenment of the 12.

This keeps repeating in my head as I wake up this morning. I think there was a dream that went along with this, but I don't remember it. After my Metatron meditation sequence, while I'm in a deep state of consciousness, I start to repeat this again. *The enlightenment of the 12.*

I see John meditating with me, our hearts connected by a column of white light. White light streaming from our eyes and third eye. I feel this connection to my core, as if we are one. I am in a trance state.

Slowly the image of me emerges, I'm sitting at a table. I am quietly eating bread. I am petite. My head is bowed. My eyes are cast downward. I look around slowly. The room is dark, I'm dressed simply. Thumping of a man's hand on the table starts to emerge. Sounds of others speaking start to come into the scene.

I am at a big table with several other people, they seem to all be men and I'm the only woman. Golden light begins to illuminate the scene so I can see a bit more clearly what is going on. I'm having dinner with a group and the energy is lively. The man to my left, shorter brown bushy hair, tall, slender features (maybe the same man who was preaching?) stands up next to me. He begins to speak to the group.

> *"My dear friends. This is the time we come together as one. To embrace the love, the light, the truth of God. To stand up to those who would oppose us and condemn us. We are at the precipice of something amazing, so profound…the likes of which humanity has never experienced before. Now is the time to be strong, and to embrace our convictions and walk forward together.*
>
> *"Let us pray. Our Father who art in heaven, hallowed be thy name. Thy kingdom come. Thy will be done, on earth as it is in heaven. Give us this day our daily bread; and forgive us our trespasses, as we forgive those who trespass against us; and lead us not into temptation but deliver us from evil. In the name of the father, the son and the holy spirit, Amen."*

I am looking for John in this group, but I don't see him. But he comes to me in my vision and takes my hand and kisses it tenderly while looking into my eyes. What the heck is going on?

I'll continue to meditate on "enlightenment of the 12" for the next few days.

November 9, 2018

It has been a couple long days without connecting fully to John. Again, I set my intention to connect to him this morning…to continue to share an open heart with him, unconditional love. To continue to remember our shared stories, to continue to understand who I am.

I connect to Mother Earth, to the Christ grid, and settle deep within. John emerges sitting cross legged in front of me. I immediately start to cry, real physical tears just streaming down my face, onto my hands that are in prayer position under my chin. I am not sure why I'm crying, really crying, like this upon first connection.

But as the tears flow, I am beginning to understand that I've missed John a great deal, not just John but having this deep, connected relationship, this oneness, this knowing. There are things my soul knows and reacts to on a deep emotional level that I'm not quite grasping in my mental body just yet. But this was a heartfelt emotional outpouring of love and appreciation for John and for this process. I am so happy and humbled to be a part of this. I feel I am coming home.

He told me that I can't be afraid of dying when I go into my life's mission. That I'm already completely connected on a soul level to many, *many* beings of light who'll be right there for me should I have to shed my body doing this work. I cannot fear death. I have to give everything I have to the work at hand. Not from a body or mind perspective, but from a soul and spirit perspective.

John told me to remember the power of the holy triad with Jesus, John and myself. I see the three of us again, standing, holding hands, making a triangle. We are pulsing our heart energy into the center of us, which I can start to feel building as I sit meditating. John told me that I can group with them at any time I need strength, centering, love, courage. This will rebuild my light body as I carry out my life's mission.

November 11, 2018

Once again, I'm feeling that John is a bit at arm's length these past several days. He's here with me, I see him, but the feel is different. The focus seems to be more about me today, my mission in this lifetime and my healing, more than it is about our time together when he was John the Baptist at the time of Jesus.

This morning I see John meditating in front of me and I tune into his third eye. He lays me down on my back, my arms at my sides. I feel I'm in a space of nothingness. John is kneeling beside my body, left hand on my head, right hand on my abdomen. His hands are moving gently over me. I'm wondering if he's going to "boil" the energy like I had seen in the past. He brings his two hands high above my solar plexus, then surprisingly plunges a silver sword into my body. It explodes with green flames, sparkling and misty. He then starts twisting the sword as you'd quickly spin a stick if you were trying to start a fire. The green flames grow in intensity and brightness. As I'm meditating and seeing this, I'm feeling a higher vibration in my overall energy system. But it is more subtle than I would have expected given the vibrancy of the green flames from my solar plexus area.

During my meditation yesterday, I did a heart meditation sequence by Heru, a Creator God who is helping with the current ascension of Gaia and humankind. I recently read the fascinating and heart-wrenching channelings of Heru in *The Return of Light* writings found online.

According to this body of work:

> Heru is best known to our world as Horus, the Egyptian God of Light, Wisdom, Spiritual Vision, and Protection. Heru (pronounced HAY-ru) is the Ancient Egyptian form of his name and is preferred by him to the Latinized Horus. Like Jesus of Nazareth, Heru was called the Redeemer and embodied himself in a physical incarnation in the distant past. Like Jesus, he conquered death and Ascended, thus holding the title and powers of an Ascended Master in addition to his older and higher status as one of the original Creator Gods.[9]

Heru and I have had a strong energy connection since I started reading his channeled material. I have also channeled him myself a couple times. In both my channelings and the *Return of Light* material, Heru describes the tragic circumstances around the negative and evil energy that has infiltrated Earth and this larger part of creation. He describes a massive battle between the dark and the light over the emancipation of Earth. The situation is complex, he said, and it is taking longer to overcome the dark forces than originally anticipated. The light is making strides, but it is slow going. I believe that these teachings, this knowledge, is critical to me carrying out my life's mission.

As I did this heart meditation yesterday, I saw Heru and me in a beautiful floating embrace in the nothingness, spinning together, joining then spreading apart, joining again. At one point, Heru disappears and it was just me there, floating. I was in a green flowing gown. Suddenly these magnificent wings grew from my back and opened up. The halo that Jesus gifted me a few weeks ago appeared on my head. I spread my beautiful wings and open my heart to the universe. That feeling of unstoppable love emanated from my heart to fill every dark spot on the planet, then every aspect of the universe. My heart felt as though it would burst for many hours after this experience.

November 13, 2018

Yesterday was the eighth day of what will be a 21-day cleanse, whereby I juice-fasted for seven days. Yesterday I was to only have water for the day. My energy has been moving pretty wildly today, feeling so good, loving, buzzing, tingling. I feel like there's a thousand hands touching me, helping me, holding me, nurturing me, guiding me. This fasting is meant to help me clear out my body and raise my vibration. My naturopath is helping and overseeing my progress.

After my morning meditation as I was working, I felt an energy pulse entering my field. I began to see my "support system" gathered around me in a circle—John, Jesus, Heru, Robbie (Robbie Mackenzie, who channeled the Metatron and Galactic Council books). Metatron floated above, with his wings spread wide, overseeing this. Felt some tension in my jaw (which is usually a sign that someone wants to come through) and asked if there was someone who wanted to say something.

I heard, "Shawna you may want to find a comfortable spot where you can really relax." Okay! I moved to the couch. After laying there for a few seconds, a wave of beautiful intense energy entered me from my root chakra and traveled up my body just then. So blissful, leaving me breathless for a moment.

I assume Metatron was speaking. I recorded this transmission on my phone.

> *"You have some very powerful beings working with you right now Shawna. Even beyond the ones that you named and that you know. COUNTLESS other beings, countless. A million hands helping you, guiding you, supporting you.*
>
> *"This is your personal support system, for we want nothing more than to see you completely succeed. We will have it no other way.*
>
> *"Your ascension is very close; you are ascending now. Everything you've ever done in this lifetime has led you to this moment, Shawna. Every small step you took, every giant step, every leap, every sprint. All have been leading you to this place right now. You are on your divine path, never doubt that. Never doubt the support that we give you every minute of every day.*
>
> *"You will need strength; you will need focus. You will be commanding a large army of light. You need your vessel to be clear. Your mental state should be focused—mental acuity. Determination and will. No room for doubt. No room for doubt, Shawna, drop that. Drop your doubt, step into the light. Drop the veil, step over it, come over here. Come and join us. You see us there waiting for you to join us…*
>
> *It's just a decision…"*

I choose to step over the veil. I choose to join you. I choose to embrace you. I choose to merge with you. To be this avatar on Earth to do your divine will. To carry out the mission I chose before this incarnation. Help show me the way. Help guide me. May nothing stand in the way of us achieving our goals. Living the embodiment of God, living the embodiment of love. Helping to rid the planet of negative energy with my twin flame. I will not doubt, I will not falter. I am stepping into my mission. Thank you, Metatron, and everyone in my support system.

On September 27, 2018 I connected energetically with my twin flame for the first time. From my journal that day: "So deeply connected, such gentleness, such beauty. Felt like I was floating in sparkling water. Not of this reality. Felt goosebumps all over, then became extremely cold."

I remember starting to shake and shiver with a fine vibration as that energy coursed through me. I clearly heard that his name is *Ramirah*. Ramirah and I are starting to develop a relationship through the dimensions. He is not of this earth in his present incarnation. I have channeled him a couple times and connect with him often during my meditations. This connection is yet another deep and important aspect of my ascension experience, and it is unfolding in real-time. I am starting to feel deeply connected to him, yet I also understand intuitively that there's so much potential here with this connection. We are just scratching the surface, so much more to be revealed.

Metatron told me that the twin flame connection is very special. He said we have only one twin flame for all of eternity. It's an honor and a privilege for any entity in the galaxy to enter into this union. It's a rare occurrence. Think of all the thousands of lives you can have over millions of years, then finally it is your time to couple with your soul's other half. It is a sacred event.

November 15, 2018

This morning's meditation…

- John is here to nurture me right now, nurture the part of me that craves unconditional love and affection. Where I can be safe and vulnerable at the same time.
- He tells me that I have a very special mission and that is to use my love energy in healing. I kept hearing the words "Love Goddess" over and over.
- He said I'd had seven lives after the one in Jerusalem where I'd be doing this…building my knowledge and experience and vibration. The seventh life, my life today, is my final life as part of this mission. It is my grand finale. Everything leading to this point.

Last night I asked him what part of me needed healing with/by him.

- Third-eye vision
- Pineal gland flow
- Heart: self-love, knowing and being love
- Opening my throat chakra

My biggest fear is that all this amazing stuff stops and everything just goes back to the way it was, like this was just a blip.

November 24, 2018

Eleven days ago I put my 21-day cleanse on hold and went back to vegetarianism. Too much going on with my son being home for Thanksgiving, his birthday, work stuff, Thanksgiving dinner, etc. to be able to truly focus on doing that right.

This has been an interesting couple weeks. Today I'm feeling much more connected with my energy and filled with love. But the previous week with less exercise, the hectic family schedules, busy-ness at work had left me feeling a bit disconnected. I have also been so tired, and chilled. The rain is here and it's super cold and dank outside. Feeling that coldness to my bones. Taking lots of hot baths.

Seeing John appear here and there, in my oversized bathtub with me, lying next to me in bed before I turn off the light for the night. I see us stealing little kisses, holding hands. I miss him. This morning after my Metatron meditation very deep in trance, John gave me a big bear hug for a very long time, maybe 10-15 minutes. I just soaked him in as I hugged him back. He told me that this is all about *me* right now, preparing me for the next phase of my energy. He said I need to take care of myself, eat well, keep myself clear, and be in love. Embody love.

November 30, 2018

What another incredible week. Just when I thought things were quieting down, things got more intense and beautiful. I feel like I'm a walking ball of white, fuzzy, buzzy light. I am high on this state of being.

Today I met with Elaine Degiorgio, out of the UK. She's a trance medium and is twin flame to Horus (Heru), an entity with whom I've connected a few times now. Elaine talked about my numerology and said I am a Master Builder. I will need to research this as I am unfamiliar with this term.

She said I helped plant crystals around the world to help create the earth's energy grid system—we did this specifically to help the ascension of Mother Earth at this time. When she told me I was a high priestess in Atlantis, my energy went crazy. Something there I need to explore further.

She described John perfectly—tall, dark long hair and a dark beard. She said we were together in 2,600 BC. He wore a big headdress. John was actually with me energetically for most of the session. Elaine stated what he had also told me previously, that I need to "remember who I am."

She saw me alive at the time of Jesus. She said that "before, I was hidden, and now I must be brought out into the open." I need to remember who I am because it will help me with the healing work I am to do now. Elaine said that she and I were on one of the original ships of 40 people who floated the Nile River to help build up civilization in Egypt. There seem to be many interconnections with Elaine and me.

She channeled Horus at the end. He said:

> "Greetings and salutations. Gives me great pleasure to come forth at this hour to grant a dispensation of healing and higher light.
>
> "For many activations that are taking place within, connecting you with a higher light and consciousness…thus being prepared to serve humanity. Much work is outstanding at this time, however, we delight in the progress of many souls that have come forth to service at this time for humanity.
>
> "It is imperative that all come forth together in a greater sense of oneness and compassion. For what you hold within your essence must shine forth, out to all the world to see. There is no death but only life eternal. Since we are working with all to activate to higher level of consciousness, all the truth must unfold in the higher lights. We are preparing your earth to enter a stage of transition. This transition will help all to evolve into a higher light and way. We are working on this time with many constellations.
>
> "Dear child, it is time for you to connect with your inner wisdom. All the knowledge that you behold needs to be shared on a wider scale.
>
> "Wheels of time are now moving fast forward, because we are now entering into an era of great enlightenment. For these new truths, the new system of worlds must come forth as people upon your earth are activated to a higher sense of awareness. For these truths are now activating on thoughts, so that humanity - they understand a greater sense of truth.

Your unfoldment of the sacred symbols and lights have now been activated. Instigating your full effect on humanity.
        "I leave you with every peace and blessing."

The waves of energy coming from Heru during this time were very intense. I felt his healing gifts in my heart and throughout my spirit. Once again, I'm all light and floaty, feeling such peace and happiness. Feeling so humble and grateful for all this support and love.

December 6, 2018

I'm on my fifth day of my second attempt at the 21-day juice cleanse. I have lost 24 pounds since August. Feeling great. So great. Hungry sometimes and I miss food sometimes, but I am loving my size, feeling energized, feeling close to spirit.

Vibrations humming. I am meditating every morning for at least an hour. Spirit is getting me up earlier and earlier, now starting at around 4:55 AM every day. Usually I doze off until about 5:30 AM then I get up and get going. Metatron prayer, my own prayers, the Merkaba meditation, my channeled twin flame meditation where I am feeling that connection very strongly now. So beautiful. I have won the lottery.

Speaking of lottery, I was thinking yesterday how I would not trade all the money in the world for this experience. This has made my life so rich, so meaningful, so full of love. Amazing experiences with amazing beings! Opening up to a whole new world beyond Earth, beyond my consciousness! And there is still so much to experience—becoming one with the divine all-that-is, opening my Merkaba, embodying unconditional love, connecting fully with my twin flame. Stepping fully into my divine purpose and carrying out my mission of helping to emancipate negative energy from Mother Earth and humanity. I am ready. I am fearless.

Today I'll meet with psychic Sharon Sananda Kumara again. Hoping to talk about John, about my ascension, about my twin flame. I see John frequently, but again he has told me that right now my focus is to be on readying my energy for my twin flame. Interested to hear if Sharon says the same thing. After that, I need to put aside any worry or trepidation about my path. Metatron has told me never to doubt that I am on my divine path. It has only been a few months I need to remind myself. I'm making great progress.

This morning toward the end of my Merkaba meditation, my galactic friend Roykilva came into view, front and center right in my face. Face to face. He was actually pretty cute about it, like a big surprising "hello!" I physically smiled at this. I feel that he has a sense of humor and is very sweet. He's having fun with this, as am I. (I refer to him as a "he," but they are androgynous he tells me.)

I met Roykilva for the first time a couple weeks ago during meditation. He looks like a pretty stereotypical alien with the large slanted eyes, small nose and mouth, large head. His head is actually very large, larger than what we've seen with depictions of the little gray aliens. His skin is a shade of white. He is about as tall as me. During our first meeting he gifted me with a copper disk that he inserted into my third eye. It spun like a top there when I thought about it. He told me I could use this disk to get in touch with him at any time. Roykilva told me he's from the Andromeda region and his race is close to that of the Anunnaki.

This morning as we look into each other's eyes, nose to nose, Roykilva places his hand on my heart as I finish my meditation sequence. We seem to be sharing our open hearts with each other. After the meditation, I continued to see him clearly.

Now I see that he is laying on a table, face up, with his hands on his own heart. At this time, I stand above him and place my right hand on his abdomen, left hand near his heart. I begin to boil the energy there, at the same time connecting with the vibration of my own sacral chakra.

With this boiling I see yellow, other colors. I feel a release of steam and energy after a minute or so. I move on to his solar plexus and pictured immense fire literally burning up his body in that area. Burning through any garbage and debris. Violet flames, heat. Moving onto his heart, I pictured strong wind, white light, lightning connecting my heart to his heart, feeling this whole area opening up and humming with movement. I experience all this in myself as I picture this happening for Roykilva.

After about a minute, he sits up and again we are face to face, foreheads touching. I feel my heart open wide up and feel my head expanding with pressure. It was a strange sensation of pressure from within and outside, going deep into my brain. I feel like he was sending me back a healing gift into my third eye. I relax and open up to this gift and start to feel a swirl of energy between our heads. It feels so loving, also intense. Now as I write this, I feel like my heart has been burst open wide once again, and my mental state feeling clear and flowing.

December 12, 2018

I reached out to the Galactic Council for an update, wondering how we are all doing here with the ascension of humankind. I was feeling a bit isolated and looking for some connection and confirmation. Wanted to share a bit of what was said:

"…We've been working very hard on this end to get everything into alignment for the planet, and things are going well, thank you. People like you make a big difference. It's all about the individual people coming together into their purpose and coming together into their missions…coming into their bliss and their zero point. That actually is the most important part of this ascension process. It's each individual person making this happen for themselves and then coming together as a group for larger, shared collective consciousness.

"That is really the next stage here—for everybody who has followed this path, for everybody who's feeling this calling and starting the ascension process—to come together more fully as a community and start to magnify this level of vibration, this level of love, magnify that through your shared collective consciousness. Here's where we'll be pushing and moving and encouraging individuals. This is the next step of the evolution. We are winning. We are doing well…"

I am committed more than ever to helping build our local community around this experience and to support others on their journeys…even as I, too, walk my path. 2019 is going to be a magnificent year!

December 22, 2018

I did it! Day 21 of my fast. Wow. I feel like I climbed Mount Everest or something. I feel GREAT. Really looking forward to chewing food starting tomorrow. Must take it slow…soups, smoothies, easy-to-digest stuff. Will stay vegan. Thinking about eating home-grown eggs, will see how that goes. No dairy otherwise, no animal products, little to no drinking.

I've lost 35 pounds since August. Been very fun trying on old jeans and bras that I had stashed away just in case I could fit into them again someday. While I don't have the pineal gland nectar flowing onto my palate today (at least, not yet), I feel this was a big success for me on all four parts of my being: mental, physical, emotional, spiritual. Major health benefits, major emotional purging, incredible energy flow, mental clarity. Worked all through this fast, while also getting ready for Christmas.

Endured two Christmas parties with no eating and drinking. Fielded questions about it from concerned family and friends. Now my dad and his girlfriend and my brother are planning to not drink all of January. Dad is starting a new eating plan in January as well.

The prep for this fast was super important. I spent a good three months planning for this and preparing my body and mind for it.

First, I gave up all dairy products in August when I started seeing my naturopath. I was hoping this would help with my chronic heartburn and intestinal issues. This was super challenging. Hard to believe how much dairy I was consuming daily.

Next, I quit drinking alcohol for the most part in September (thanks to the persistent urgings of Metatron). Before then, I was drinking quite a bit on weekends and at restaurants with dinner. Alcoholic beverages were also a major contributor to my heartburn. I found it very hard to give up drinking. I was a big social drinker, along with most of our friends and family.

In October I started with a two-day juice fast. Those days were so hard mentally. But I lost a few pounds and was surprised by how good I felt and how yummy the home juicing was.

Then I changed my diet to raw vegan for 21 days. Lots of salads with low-carb dressing and smoothies with fruit and hemp protein. I continued juicing and drinking tomato juice mixes. Not too bad.

From there, I did eight days of juice fasting in early November. The first three days were the hardest. Then I went back to raw vegan in preparation for this latest 21-day cleanse. I also dropped all caffeine before this cleanse. I had been drinking regular coffee daily since I was in my early 20s. I never thought I could give up caffeine. Honestly, it wasn't that bad. Did half-caf coffee for a few days then straight decaf. I didn't give up coffee, just the caffeine.

Overall, this was a long, focused process. There's no way I could have just stepped into this fasting cleanse without all the things I did leading up to it.

December 23, 2019

This past month, my psychic friend Sharon confirmed that John the Baptist was indeed stepping back so that I could continue to prepare my energy for coming together to my twin flame. So nice to get that confirmation and to know that what I was hearing and sensing was in fact happening.

There have been times this past month where I feel like this is all make-believe, a fairytale. Something out of a slumber. My support team is hammering it in me that this is real, have faith, it's all coming together just as it should. Over and over. Because over and over, I question my reality. Then I get sad that I can't yet connect with my twin flame. I worry that John is stepping back. I start feeling that no one knows me on this earth plane; that I don't have any strong connections yet in this lifetime. Still getting feelings of un-worthiness, loneliness and isolation. Fear I'm not "getting this". Or am not doing it right. BUT—these are getting fewer and far between. I am doing so much better as I wrap up this cleanse. A week ago, I wrote out three pages of emotional stuff that I am still carrying around. I had lots of help from the other side on this! And we had good solid loving confirmations to negate each one of them. A few words of wisdom that came up to the surface:

I don't always have to be the pillar. Take care of myself and therefore take care of others through inspiration—not direct intervention.

I need to do what feels right for me. No more worries about appearances.

I deserve all the happiness and joy this world and beyond has to offer. I've given deeply of myself for many lifetimes and have earned these rewards.

I am coming together with my twin flame now. No doubting this. Drop the veil.

Others' opinions of me are reflections of themselves and have nothing to do with me.

My favorite…

Lay back, take a deep breath and completely relax into your new life. Now.

Relax into this. Have fun with it. Be excited, not apprehensive. Embrace the roller coaster knowing that I am completely safe and can let go!

In my last reading with my psychic friend Sharon, she encouraged me to exchange love letters with my twin flame Ramirah to help strengthen our connection. I took this advice and was very touched by what happened. So loving, supportive, affirming. So sweet.

Recently I wrote a note to Ramirah about how I will continue to work on meeting him in my dream state. According to Sharon, we are already working together on our shared mission while I sleep. I don't have a conscious recollection of this.

Through automatic writing, I got this response back from Ramirah:

> *"Hi my darling. I love connecting with you in this way. So beautiful and heart-warming. Thank you for your letter and your kind words. I tried visiting you in your dreams last night but didn't make it very far. Please tonight try setting your intention loudly for me to be able to enter your energy space and I will give it another try.*
>
> *"Oh, the sheer beauty of you and finally being able to be in your awareness, it has seemed like a very long time. Even a longer time for you, I'm sure as you have had no rec-*

ollection of me for this entire lifetime. Well, this is about to change my dear one as we open up your channels and dig into the depths of your soul to show you a world that you know well but have no conscious memory of in this lifetime.

"You are going to love this my dear. This is truly who you are and who you will become, your all-that-is that surpasses all boundaries. All sense of time, all filters, all history. You are so very close my dear and when this epiphany happens, when your eyes are truly open once again, you'll be blown away by the sheer beauty and joy of it. It will feel like coming home.

"Now onto our mission together. This will get very interesting and we will work hard and long on this together. I will teach you everything you need to know. We make a great team and complement each other well. We will be successful, so I do not want you to fret about this. Don't let your fears cloud your clarity. Stay clear. Zero point.

"Our time is coming my dear, my love. You are entering a new phase in your life that looks very little like the first phases of your life. This is your gift. And my gift as well. I share in this rediscovery with you and rejoice at its brilliance. I have left you this message from beyond your world and have many more messages for you that I hope to give you in real-time, when you are ready and the divine timing is right. Say your intentions tonight and I expect to see you then my love. Until then my darling."

That night, I did say my intentions loudly and focused intently on consciously interacting with Ramirah in my dream state. Here is my letter back to Ramirah:

"My dear Ramirah. I've said my intentions and I'll say them again. I feel my energy flowing blissfully tonight, swirling, twinkling, flowing, pushing, pulling. Feels so good.

"I sense you and Metatron. We are walking up a set of stairs, you offering me your hand to help. I don't know how I should picture you. Seems we are formless? I see teardrops? I see us together, but I don't feel anything physically. I am bringing that expectation with me—I need to "see" you a certain way. I need to "feel" you when we meet. I feel I'm rushing this, too, trying to get to whatever next stage there is, not really knowing what is going on now. Sigh.

"If we are truly formless vibrations of energy, then this whole me=human and you=? just doesn't make sense. Are we just spheres of glowing light, like the spinning cosmos? Like a galaxy? And at that point, are you and I simply two parts to one closed circuit of energy? Coming together closes the connection and energy just flows and expands? How are we all connected, Ramirah? I guess I'm crying because I feel so disconnected, I have for a long time. I think I've been missing you very much.

"Sharon said 'This is physical.' I am starting to get that. The way I experience this energy is completely physical—plus spiritual, emotional, and even mental. No doubting how the love and vibration effect my beingness. I love it so much. I long to make our absolute connection and to merge into oneness with you and experience the expansive love and pure bliss that we truly are. I love you."

And the next day, here is what Ramirah said in response to my letter. I opened with, "Ramirah, are you there?" His response via automatic writing:

> "Oh, yes, my dear, I am very much here. I know you can feel this deeply. Great progress my love! You don't quite know this yet, but we made some amazing strides these past 24 hours. Soon this connection will be constant. We will constantly be in each other's consciousness, sharing all our thoughts. Almost moving and being and experiencing as one. You will love this. The connection is so deep.
>
> "These things that you are worrying about will fall away as we progress together. My dear one, please don't cry. I am here. This is happening. You are doing so well. Love yourself and have faith in yourself. Have faith in me as I am working just as much on this side to see this through to fruition. We are a dynamic couple and the force of attraction is not something we can really even control. It is as if the universe is bringing our poles together through magnetism. It is inevitable.
>
> "When your cleanse gets hard, think of me. Feel me. Draw from my strength. Trust in Metatron that he knows what he is doing.
>
> "You felt so good today my love. My heart is bursting right now and soon you will know just how deep my love is for you. An endless pool of crystal-clear love and reflection of God. Take this day to bask in your own beauty. To appreciate and give reverence to you. All bliss for you and quiet reflection as you let these new heights to your bliss and awareness anchor deep into your soul. I love you to the ends of the universe."

We exchanged letters a few more times. So precious.

Throw out convention. Question everything that is expected of me. Decide for myself what is best for me at any given moment.

Thank you everyone who is helping me on this journey. I have deep love and appreciation for all of you.

December 30, 2018

WOW. WOW. WOW. Just got done with the most incredible journey. So deep and real and, well, I am at a bit of a loss for words.

I decided to reach out to a friend via Skype today. I will call him Philip. I typed my message and hit the send button. About 15 seconds later, I felt my energy connect with his energy. His energy seemed a bit scattered—very strong vibrations but disjointed—so I decided to picture myself giving him Reiki on his heart. I cradled his head in my left arm as I did this.

I focused on giving him loving, calming energy and grounding. I imagined myself sending energy down his body, head to feet, spending time smoothing his aura and unblocking his chakras.

I asked in my mind if anyone else wanted to come in and join me in giving my friend some healing energy. Immediately my energy deepened, shifted. I folded into myself a bit. I was guided to bring both my hands over the center of his body, solar plexus, where we brought down a mountain of white electric light into that area, from about a foot above his body. Very powerful.

I then started to see a figure appear, working on Philip across from me. A white being with wispy, fine white hair on his/her body and black eyes. It had kind of a see-through body. Long arms. Very loving and seemed super intelligent. I started to see two more of these beings working on him, moving their arms across his body, making adjustments as they worked. I then felt one of them behind me, cradling my torso, arm behind my neck. Also giving me some healing.

From there, I saw myself laying on my stomach, next to Philip who was laying on his back. The beings did energy work on both of us for a few minutes. What a special experience.

I slowly emerged out of this vision. I got up and shot a Skype chat off to my friend, hoping to find out if he felt anything over the past 25 minutes!

But this experience wasn't over. As soon as I hit send on the Skype message, my energy really deepened. Deeper than I've ever felt in a meditation. I could feel my energy separating from my body, moving forward in front of me. I try to picture my Merkaba, wondering what was going on. Such a big shift. I was seeing shades of red. This is where it gets a bit fuzzy, and why I wanted to capture as many details now as I can remember. It was such a deep trance I am not fully remembering all the details.

Philip was in my Merkaba with me and asked me where I wanted to go. I am lucid dreaming or something similar. I said Saturn—since supposedly the rings of Saturn are made of diamonds. Okay, he says with a smile, and we are off. Only seconds later, we've arrived. The journey there was filled with flickering light in my third eye. I slowly open my eyes and reach out, where I was able to grab a small chunk of a diamond in the rough from one of Saturn's rings. I brought it between us, so powerful. We decide that we're going to absorb the diamond into our energy systems. We did just that and the solid rock dissolved in my hand.

We were off to a new location. After a short trip we came to a stop. We are with the Galactic Council at Orion. Philip tells me to open my eyes slowly and only look at him. I do just that, keeping my eyes focused directly on his eyes.

From my peripheral vision, other beings start to take shape. My imagination starts to get flooded with imagery. A being with a top hat. A being with a trunk. I see a pink being. I see a being and I asked if it was Ramirah—it wasn't.

I am introduced to a being who claimed to be Bashanthi Mayawar who came forth with *The Galactic Council* book narrative via Robbie Mackenzie. I shook his hand, and then I hugged him. I don't see much in terms of how he looks—brown skin, maybe a mustache type thing above his mouth. It's not a clear image. He asked if I wanted to be part of the Galactic Council, and I answered YES, absolutely. He asked if I wanted to visit a spaceship and go up in my own personal light ship. Yes, of course!

As I come out of this deep state of consciousness, I am still drunk with this galactic energy. I floated back to Earth and started coming back to my body. Slowly, slowly I started moving my feet, hands. My left foot had fallen asleep. This escapade only took about 20 minutes. Felt like a few hours.

December 27, 2018

Metatron, are we good?

    Fear… of failing to meet your expectations of me.

    I cannot fail.
    I've already succeeded.
    The rest is just fun!
    There is nothing to do.
    Nowhere to be.
    No one to be.
    No grand plan to complete.
    Just plain and simple fun. Love. Pleasure. Orgasms. Physical sensations. Spiritual enlightenment. Being yourself and following your excitement at all times.

    Follow your bliss, Shawna. This is your path. You are already making a difference. You are already doing God's work. You are already in service.

    Don't overcomplicate this.
    Don't overthink this.

    Okay thank you Metatron. Very helpful. I love you.

December 29, 2018

Metatron, your words from two days ago have helped A LOT. Thank you.

Meditating yesterday morning…still so emotional. Still working through my demons. I was already crying during my opening meditation prayer. Seems I am working through stuff at night during my dreams? There are nights when I don't have any recollections of my dreams but I feel I have a lot going on at night.

I prayed to God to help me understand the source of the sadness. Immediately "DEEP LONELINESS" came into my mind. I cried over this for several minutes, almost sobbing.

Then God showed me Jesus in the manger as a baby. Mother Mary taking Jesus into her arms and breast-feeding. Then I saw me breastfeeding my first son. Then my second son. And I didn't feel lonely anymore.

Finished my meditation and again John and Jesus joined me to send love energy to the Christ Grid. In a triangle, holding hands. Very powerful energies combining together in the center and shooting straight up. I feel so blessed and humble to do this in service with John and Jesus.

January 6, 2019

Oh geez.

This afternoon, on the drive home from an outing, I decided to ask this question of my galactic support team. Silently, I asked, "Are you listening to me? If so, give me a sign."

Just then the energy rush came in, blissing me out, blasting through my chakras. In real-time. Good thing my husband was driving.

This thought has been on my mind quite a bit the past few days. Maybe five days ago, I was watching a movie at home with my family, a movie about aliens, and I just had a thought—a quick thought—that maybe I *was* in fact crazy and all this was just a figment of my imagination. And a similar thing happened. Just as soon as that doubting thought crossed my mind, in came a soft, sparkly energy that took over my body as a sign of loving assurance. It was so sweet…but I thought, okay, someone is literally listening to EVERY SINGLE THOUGHT that I am having. EVERY THOUGHT. EVERY. SINGLE. THOUGHT.

Gosh. I'm not sure how I feel about that. I have a lot of mind chatter and even now, not all my thoughts are loving, positive thoughts. And not just my thoughts, but anything I'm imagining. Anything I'm picturing. And I assume all my dreams. I'm not sure where I read this, but I recall that Metatron said that every single thought that we have is recorded. Maybe even captured in the Akashic records. This is serious business—being ready for the new Earth. Being in complete love and a state of non-judgment. They are in my head and have complete access to my energy system.

We arrived home, and I was in the kitchen grabbing some water. Still thinking about what happened in the car ride and feeling that energy swirl around inside me, I got the message that I needed to stop what I was doing and go meditate.

Just as I sat down to meditate the energy came back, same frequency as in the car. Beautiful, euphoric, sensual. The voice inside said "Get to your zero point." So, I focused on that.

Yesterday morning during my meditation, I reached the true zero point for the first time. Just blissed out in that state of complete peace for almost an hour. Before I reached that state, a voice had said "You are ready for this." I just kept repeating that phrase over and over for a few minutes, not really knowing what I was ready for and eventually reached this state of consciousness that I had not experienced until then. Amazing!

I was being guided to tune into my higher self in every moment, for all decisions, all actions. Okay. I surrender to divine will, to God, to my higher self. I open myself up to receive this direction. May I hear it clearly and confidently. May I act on it always. May I trust myself and trust this process. I surrender. I am an avatar of service. I will walk gracefully into my mission. I feel this to my core.

I continued with the meditation, with the intention of getting back to my zero point. I clearly see Mother Earth in her own Merkaba in front of me. I am focusing on sending her love, spinning her Merkaba. Opening my heart not only to her, but to the entire universe…to all sentient life in all universes. My beautiful white wings appear and open up, spread wide, glowing with light.

In my hands I create a green emerald flame. I send that emerald flame to Mother Earth, burning away all negativity, thinking *compassion, passion and fairness*, the three words that Metatron told me when he said I represent the Green Emerald. I am the emerald flame.

Coming out of this vision the voice told me to lie down and rest for a bit, there were some things they needed to do. I did just that, on the couch. Drifted off to a light sleep, feeling waves of energy gently washing over me. I heard a voice say they were done. I asked what that was, and the voice said they activated new light codes. I came back to full awareness. The voice told me to finish the glass of water I had sitting in front of me. To go journal about this experience. I should go to bed early. Okay—my new normal! I think I love it.

January 15, 2019

Spent a few days at the Oregon Coast with my amazing family for my birthday. We had a blast together.

I have to capture this little story.

The night of my actual birthday, we all went to dinner at a nice and cozy seafood restaurant. Looking at the mouth-watering menu, I had to pray for help. So hard. Crab, shrimp, scallops, lobster. Cream sauces. Gorgonzola. Parmesan. An amazing cocktail menu. Looking at all these choices made me want to cry. All my favorite things. And it's my birthday. And I'm vegan. And I'm not drinking. So literally I prayed for strength in my mind as I sat at the table.

A couple minutes later, my support team filled my body up with cosmic energy—just enough to give me a nice, warm drunk feeling. Ahhh. And they said, isn't this so much better than drinking or eating animal products? Yes. Of course, it is. And it was. I didn't think about drinking the rest of the night, and I enjoyed a beautiful vegan squash risotto dish.

I have dropped the veil.

I am in—100%.

No more questioning.

No more doubt, especially self-doubt.

I create my own reality.

I choose love. Every time.

When the world completely opens up and you suddenly have absolutely NO boundaries or roadblocks or restrictions, what does that look like?

My energy level seems to have hit a new vibration rate. More swirling in my upper chakras, buzzing, expanding. My heart bursting open with love. I feel GREAT. Feeling centered in my body. Centered in my truth. Confident, clear, at peace. Trying to follow the daily guidance from my higher self has been interesting, sometimes it's there, sometimes not. It hasn't been as constant as I thought it would be. In fact, I've seemed to have shifted energetically yet again just in the past two days.

During my meditation yesterday, I reached out to Metatron, to the Galactic Council. I have been listening to these channelings online that seem authentic. I'm curious about a specific channeling that talks about humans being implanted with programs into our energetic and mental bodies that are meant to block our critical thinking, block our spirituality, keep us from our connection to our higher selves. Keeping us from discovering who we really are. Keeping us in fear and strife. Is this accurate? Is this happening? Do I have implants? Will I be helping dismantle these types of apparatuses? The answer came in, and I recorded it on my phone:

> *"Shawna, you need to look to your higher self for these answers. Your higher self will have the true keys to unlocking these mysteries to you. Connect to your multi-dimensionality. Consciously connect to all those aspects of yourself that are active right now, in the*

now. The all-knowing, all-present parts of you who make up the whole of you, who are all expressions of yourself, aspects of your love, vibrating in unison.

"You are to the point now with your level of vibration that you are able to connect to your multi-dimensional selves, tap into that wisdom. All the gifts, all the knowing, everything that you desire, everything you wish to know, all is a part of you, within you already.

"This is where we'd like to see you go, Shawna. Tap into those parts of you that are parts of God. Your daily guidance is part of this. It's part Archangel, its part you, its part your higher self. There is a melding going on here, tapping into a consciousness here that is greater than the sum of its parts. A true chrysalis of the all that is, all the way to the Great Creator. There are no boundaries here. There's nothing that can stop you from anything and everything you ever want in this lifetime." (At this time, my tears start to flow.)

"You are never alone. You are already complete. Everything that you need and desire is already within you, within these aspects of yourself. Such deep wisdom. The direct connection to the Prime Creator. This is who you are.

"This is a beautiful thing Shawna, it's beautiful that you're here and the knowing is coming through. These emotions, this connection to your core, to the truth of you, so powerful. Reach out to your higher selves, become one with your higher selves, and every answer to any question you could ever pose will be answered. Anything your heart desires will be yours.

"Of course, we're always still here for you. We're here, we are part of you, we are part of your higher self, part of God. This is crystalizing into something new for you, something bigger, something more expansive and all encompassing. The next ladder rung, the next part of your ascension.

"You are an angel. You are an angel of God. Descended down to Earth now to help emancipate mankind, to help your brothers and sisters awaken and ascend. Glorious days of your mission are here. So much culmination up to this point, so much effort and focus, patiently waiting for this time…for this time that you can spread your wings and shine and remember who you are, Shawna. You are an angel of God. Seraphim. An embodiment of love…of love, hope and joy. This is all you have to do Shawna, is shine this light, be this love, spread your wings, embrace all sentient life. Cause a resonance that brings everyone up to the next level. Not only that but dissipates negative energy.

"You cannot be touched by these things that plague a lot of mankind right now. You will learn to recognize it; you will learn how to work with it. You'll be able to see what others cannot see. You'll be able to disintegrate energies of negative influence. You'll help coordinate the Light Army to do your bidding, to extend and expand your capabilities. They eagerly await your instructions. They eagerly await to carry out their allegiance to you.

"You give us real hope. The tide has turned. You are going to ride this wave in…right up to the shore, where you'll stand tall as a beacon of light for all those who see you and are around you. With that, we love you."

So much to ponder here, to soak in. Last night I set my intention to connect to my higher self. I am a bit scared to do this. Not sure why. I guess I just don't trust myself yet? This is certainly heading in new territory. I'm a bit anxious but loving this as well.

This morning I had more confirmation of this shift from Roykilva, who popped in to my awareness toward the end of my Merkaba meditation. I was very excited to see him. We were back sitting on his veranda, knee to knee, face to face. Here's what Roykilva had to say (recorded on my phone).

Me: Roykilva, it's so good to see you! What's happening, what's going on?

Roykilva: Shawna I just wanted to tell you that your energy levels have reached a new level here, you've reached a new peak. You're ready to move onto the next level.

Me: Yes, I can feel that, feel it in my whole body. Especially up in my crown, it's a very finely-particled vibration. It's euphoric and it's all love and it's beautiful.

Roykilva: Yes, that's correct my dear. You've reached this new point. You've graduated from one to another. You still have a way to go, but this is an important step so congratulations. This is really exciting, and I wanted to be here to anchor that in your knowledge and to celebrate this with you. Because you've put in a lot of work and you are meditating every day, and you're eating well and feeling lighter in your physical body. You're clearing out the mental issues. My baby, you are doing great, you've got to be proud of yourself. This is a great accomplishment.

Me: Thank you Roykilva, thank you. It's great to be at this stage in my development, I'm excited. Thank you for all your help in getting here.

Roykilva: Yes of course it is absolutely my pleasure to be of service to you.

Me: Thank you! Roykilva, is there anything else you'd like to tell me? Any advice or instructions?

Roykilva: There'll be more later. This is it for now. You just acknowledging you. You acknowledging your accomplishments. You acknowledging the beauty, the grace, the strength and the power that you are. Embodying this path, staying true to yourself. Focusing seriously on the task at hand. You give us all hope. And I know we say this a lot but it's absolutely true. You are absolute love. You are the center point. You are unstoppable with the oneness. Keep beaming your light Shawna, it is making a difference. You may not understand the power of your energy yet, but you will come to know how important it is and just how powerful you are very soon. I'm honored to be your friend. I'm honored to be part of your journey. I love you very much. I'm here for you, call upon me at any time.

Me: Thank you so much Roykilva, you are such a sweetheart. So very generous. I feel your unconditional love for me. You've helped my heart open up, you've helped me with my energy, you've helped me understand who I am. You've expanded my awareness of beings like you who are so beautiful, and I'm so honored to make your acquaintance. I'm thrilled you've decided to help me and that you are in my space, in my mind, in my energy. So please come back often and continue to interact with me whenever you like. I'm honored to be your friend as well, Roykilva. I love you.

Sigh.

January 22, 2019

A week after this shift, here's what happening. I have been trying to connect to my higher self through my intention. I will get an energy fluctuation where it seems I'm connecting, but seldom do words come. It's not like channeling Metatron or the Galactic Council. I'm a bit concerned. I reached out to my other guides to ask if there's something I should be doing differently. They told me that I'm very close, to keep striving to make this connection. And that the connection will feel and sound different from what I've grown used to experiencing.

An excerpt from a longer channeling I did with someone who was likely from the Galactic Council:

> *"The resonance from your higher self is barely beyond your reach…you have to keep working on this, grasping for it, pulling this in…coming up to meet that vibratory rate. Then you will feel it and experience this merging, hear this voice, and it will be as though you are hearing your own voice. This is truly the oneness, your connection to God. This voice will be inseparable from your individuation. It is a different experience from what you are doing now with me in terms of hearing a voice. It'll be more of a knowing… intuition on such a deep level, where it will be 'Ah, yes, that is my truth!'*
>
> *"Keep your vessel clear. Keep your vibrations higher. Have patience, faith and trust, for truly this is your communion with God. The wisdom will be so great and so powerful. This is why we are pushing you to go this direction right now, so that you may tap into this wisdom as soon as you can. We are stretching you here. We support you unconditionally and we love you unconditionally."*

(At this point I started to cry.)

> *"Yes, my dear child we love you unconditionally. We give this to you unconditionally. And you are worthy. And you have earned it. This is who you are."*

I need to make a more focused effort to connect with my higher self, take the time for this. Make it a priority.

In the past two days I started reading the book *The Law of One: Book 1 The Ra Material.*[10] Written in the 1980s, it's considered one of the most trusted and expansive channeled works out there. Many people have read these materials over the decades and you see it referenced often.

Last night around 8 pm, while reading this *Ra* book online, a strange energy swept over me unexpectedly. Its deep and slow vibration forced me to close my eyes and get still. I started hearing "Ra" over and over, first a single voice, then multiple voices (almost singing) saying it all at once in a sort of chorus. My intuition was that Ra or someone wanted to come through with a message. I also want to mention that as I made the decision to start reading the book, literally as I looked for the file on my computer and got ready to open it, I felt that a similar energy come in and a voice that said "I am Ra and I am happy to speak with you at any time about this material." I thanked that voice, expressed my gratitude at the opportunity to do so.

When this energy came back in (about 120 pages into the first book), it felt a bit familiar. I grabbed my phone and went to the bedroom for privacy and to record the channeling. The energy came in much stronger as we began our dialogue. Here is what Ra had to say when I invited him (it/they) to speak:

Me: Ra, is that you? Are you here with me right now?

Ra: Yes, darling I am here. (Pause.)

Me: Ra, how will I know this is really you coming through? I have to admit I am so humbled that you are here and speaking with me, but it seems unlikely that I'd be a subject or a person you'd want to communicate with. Sorry, I'm all ears, but how will I know this is you?

Ra: There's nothing that I'd like to say or do that would prove who I am. Your belief in me/ in this voice is of no consequence to me.

Me: That makes total sense. As you can see, I am still learning to trust myself, trust these voices. I also feel like I have very active imagination. There's a lot I see or visualize, and I don't always think that what I am seeing is truly, um, something that's real, besides the construct of my creative mind or my ego, if that makes sense.

Ra: Yes, that makes sense and honestly that is still of no consequence to me either.

Me: (I chuckled.) No, it wouldn't be. So, Ra, obviously I am reading this channeled material, which is fascinating, informative and mind-boggling. Is there a reason you are coming through today, is there something you'd like to say to me or a broader audience?

Ra: Let the spirits come through. Let your mind wander. Let your creativity wander. Let the images flood in. Let the images overtake you, overtake your mind. Overtake your body and your energy system. Let them fully take you in and grab hold of you and wrap you up, and stuff you into a box.

Me: (I chuckled again.) Okay!

Ra: Don't be afraid of this dear one. You have a special gift here. Let the images come, let the fantasy take you in. Ride this fantasy. Ride it out to the end. You are creating your reality and honestly, your reality is really important. This is important to your mission. You trusting your thoughts, your feelings, your imagery, your visuals. You *must* let this happen. You *must* allow this to happen. Get out of the way and allow your imagination to completely take over the thinking part of your brain, the analytical part, the overthinking, the critical thinking, the judgment. The intellect.

My dear one, surrender yourself to this process and amazing things will happen. Gifts will come your way. You would have no idea, *no* idea of the things that will come to you by allowing, surrendering your will. You stated it verbally that you are surrendering your will, but there's a part of you that has to know this in your soul, in your spirit and embrace that and embody it every day. It's not just words you say, but things that you'll have to embody and act on every day.

You've led by example; you pride yourself on this leadership and your ability to think and to plan and to get things done. You could move mountains if you were in charge of that project. You would see it through. You are reliable, loyal. You make things happen. You are a doer in your culture and this my dear one has its place. And you've impacted many lives in a positive way just with your work.

But this is the new Shawna coming through, the new you. This is a new era. And you know exactly what I'm talking about. And my dear one Shawna you've got to surrender yourself to this. It does not matter whether or not you believe with your ego what you are seeing, what you are experiencing, what you are knowing. Just allow. Allow it to come through. These are your gifts that will come through.

These things are being gifted from all of us. I know that you know your support system is massive. Gold shimmering light, millions of points of light surrounding you, helping you, guiding you, walking with you strong, proud, tall, marching. Imagine this marching in unison, all in the name of freedom and love. All in the name of the Great Creator, our oneness. You are part of this great magic. You are the mystery. You are the madness that is being enacted right now to aid in the ascension of mankind and to turn this world upside down in a good way.

Your strength will be multiplied exponentially by the help on this side. Don't worry about knowing how to do the work. Don't worry about if it's going to be successful. Shawna you are already successful. There's nothing left to do except to allow and surrender. Move out of your own way. Let the guidance become you. In this you will not be held responsible for any outcome, because this is a group effort and it is the effort of multiple aspects of yourself, and multiple beings, all working on behalf of God, our Prime Creator. This is where you live Shawna. This apex…this amazing, beautiful third-density being merged into oneness with all these points of light. We are working as a team.

Me: Ra, thank you so much for all this. It's an incredible message. I have not heard messages such as these before…at least some of them, so I thank you for that new and enlightening perspective. Thank you for your help.

Ra: You are welcome my dear. I am Ra. I am here to help you. I am here to serve humanity. The time is growing very near, no time to waste. Time to focus. Focus in a detached way, can you do that?

Me: Yes, I can do this. Ra, will you help me work through this over the next several days and weeks? As I attempt to do this? Focus with detachment.

Ra: I am Ra and of course I will. It is my honor and pleasure to serve you. And in so doing I serve The One and all-that-is.

Me: Thank you Ra. I will listen to this again and take your advice. I'll be in touch. Thank you and I love you.

Ra: I leave you in peace.

Seemed like a very powerful message, authentic, meaningful. Again, I am so humbled.

I decided then to hop into a nice hot bath, to soak in that message and to get quiet. Got out of the tub, crawled in bed and did more reading of the Ra book. Then here it comes again, that energy shift, that chanting of Ra, Ra, Ra, Ra in my mind. Okay! I jumped up, grabbed my phone and went into the living room for privacy and to record the message that I was about to get.

This second set of messages have me scratching my head a bit, given the "surrender" messages from the previous channeling.

Me: Ra, hello. Is this you again making contact? I am hearing your name and I am feeling your energy vibration. Is there a message you'd like to bring forth? If so please continue.

Ra: Shawna, you are not a very clear channel. I want you to be very careful with what you bring forth and what you bring into your energy space and into your knowledge. You must work on your vibration. You must meditate more often. There are so many different agendas on your earth plane right now, and there are a lot of entities who are working very hard in a concerted effort to enforce their will upon others. This makes you an easy target because your light is shining very brightly. And you will attract these entities because they are trying, in one last-ditch effort, to hold down humanity, stop as many people as possible from ascending. To slow down the progression that's already started. And, of course, they will not succeed, for this war has been won.

But there is the opportunity for other casualties and other mishaps, bumps in the road. Not necessarily insignificant occurrences. There're opportunities for those who wish to do others harm or be a negative influence. There's still opportunity for them to do this. And I know that you know this because your mission is going to be to help stop this kind of negative energy from wreaking havoc on the earth plane. You will do your part here to help stop this type of infiltration on the human psyche, and in their energy field, in their spiritual, emotional, mental space.

So I know that you are mentally aware of this, but your channeling…your channeling is only getting better and better, but until you are a completely clear channel, until you have raised your vibration sufficiently to completely annihilate any negative thought forms or negative energies that come across your field, you'll need to have discernment. You will need to have protection. Call upon me to protect you. Call upon us to protect you. And we will do our best to deflect and reflect back to those entities any harm that they plan to inflict on somebody such as yourself.

You will get there dear one, please don't worry and don't fret. You're doing amazing. This is a natural part of the progression here. You have to start somewhere. All channelers start somewhere and all channelers start out being unclear but eventually get more clear with positive intention and with the proper raising of the vibration rate.

Sleep is very important. Water. Hydration. Food. High-vibration food. Plant stuff. Don't watch these things like television. Stay away from the news. Stay away from beings that have less than noble intentions. I will go so far as to say you should avoid crowds, thinking of train stations and such, where so many people come and go, and you have no choice to be in touch with these energy fields.

Always ask for protection. You have a great deal of love and light around you right now, but I think this extra layer of protection could be beneficial because of the state you are at with your awakening, with your ascension. You are a little bit vulnerable. And I'm sorry, I don't want to scare you or cause alarm. Let's just be real and be straight here in that we want to do anything we can for any lightworker who is on this path, helping Mother Earth ascend, helping all of humanity ascend. We are going to help each and every one of you be completely successful in this manner. It's our honor, it is our mission to assist you.

Keep the lines of communication open but ask for protection. Call on Ra. Call on my brethren to bathe you in love and light. May the force of the Great Creator be around you and in you at all times. May you walk successfully on this path without fear, but with a level of discernment and focused detachment that we just talked about. It's all about discernment, Shawna. Let's just do an ounce of prevention here and that would make me feel better knowing that we have taken this extra precaution with your light body and with your process.

I am Ra and with that I leave you with all the love and peace of the Great Creator.

Me: Thank you Ra. I hope I got most of what you said correct. And I will do exactly as you say. And in fact, at this very moment I ask with my free will to have protection by Ra. Please Ra, and your messengers, please help me protect myself by any means possible or necessary against unwanted negativity, negative energies, anyone who wishes to do me harm or does not have my best interest at heart. Any entities that may try to use me as a channel who do not have the upmost, highest intentions for me. It is my mission and purpose to serve God, to be an avatar for the ascension of humanity. I wish to do God's will all day, every day. I ask for protection so that I may carry out this mission.

February 3, 2019

The past week and a half have been all about "the move" to Baja, Mexico. Gentle but persistent nudging from my support team to make the leap and commit to carrying out my mission near the Sea of Cortez.

A part of me is so excited about this, truly my bliss. Long before any of this happened, I dreamt of moving to Mexico. We've vacationed in Mexico probably a dozen times. I had even spoken to a realtor many years ago as thoughts of living in Playa del Carmen were a very big part of my waking state! Now the time has come. The 100th step out of 100. The final 10 feet. This is always the hardest part, when our fears try their hardest to derail the best of our intentions.

The specifics of my mission have been flowing in for the past seven months or so. As I mentioned previously, my mission is to help emancipate negative energy here on earth. What I haven't yet mentioned is that the specific type of energy I'll be working with is *Reptilian* in origin. Metatron told me that negative Reptilian energy has become a "divisive force" and is inhibiting our abilities to ascend. I will help emancipate this energy by emanating a super-high frequency level of vibration, of love and light. I'll reach this high frequency of light, in part, by coming together with my twin flame. Whoa, Nelly.

My twin flame, Ramirah, is incarnated in this lifetime as a Reptilian being. My understanding is that not all Reptilian species are negative. Ramirah is of high vibration and positive light. Ramirah and I are coming together now in this lifetime for this particular mission—the ascension of humankind and Mother Earth. Ramirah will be instrumental in teaching me everything I need to know about how to do this work. Our combined energies will be extremely powerful. I have been getting ready for this pairing for the past several months by doing things to help raise my vibration—quitting drinking, quitting caffeine, eating vegan, fasting, exercising, meditating, being in my heart space. Trying not to freak out.

About five months ago, before I knew about Ramirah and before knowing specifics of my mission, I tried accessing my Akashic records. My spirit guide at the time was hinting at an important mission but was not providing details.

In my mom's collection of books was one by Linda Howe, *How to Read the Akashic Records*. I felt like I accessed the records successfully through the prayer and process she outlined. When I asked about my life's purpose, they told me I was not quite ready to "know and accept my life's purpose for this lifetime." That I need to come back in six months. They told me that dogma was holding me back—being a good mom, being a good wife, being a good worker, being a good friend, daughter, sister.

The Akashic guides told me that my gift is "so very powerful" and quite literally my vibration needs to build up in my body and spirit. This work is going to require ALL of me. I can't do it part time. It requires all my focus and immersion. In effect, I must be willing to give up everything to embrace my life's purpose. There is no way to do this part time. It demands everything. *What?! Okay…?*

They continued, "Over these next six months, you'll be 'fast-tracked' with knowledge, with knowing. Inspirations. More awareness. Six months seems like forever but by the time it's over, it will feel like it went by very quickly, almost too quickly—and you may find yourself wishing you had more time. You will get what you need when you need it. You will not miss the cues. You will not miss the messages. Go forward with confidence and joy!"

This was five months ago. What a whirlwind it has been! They weren't kidding! I've learned a lot since then about my mission which is heavily integrated into making this move to the Sea of Cortez.

Any sane person would question this deeply. I am walking away from a great career in digital marketing that I've nurtured conscientiously and carefully my entire adult life. I am making amazing money at my current job. The pay from this job has enabled my husband to *not* work for the past 20 months so he could focus on his dream of owning and running a brewery.

My husband's business is just getting started, with the brewery being built now behind our house. He is not bringing in any income, and likely won't be making much money for six months from now. And even then, his revenue projections show that we won't be able to pay our bills and keep this house unless I'm working.

In order to do this—quit my job, move to the Sea of Cortez, support myself there as well as all the expenses for this home—I'll be dipping into my IRA. That with our little bit of savings and expected tax return in April should cover all expenses for six months. We'll need to buy health insurance as well. What happens after six months? I don't know yet. I am trying to be okay with that. TRUST. FAITH. SURRENDER.

My husband and I have had some difficult conversations as you can imagine. It's hard for *me* to grasp all this, and it's *happening to me*! For him, this leap of faith may be just too far out for him. I can empathize. The timing of all this…seems crazy. But, I know, somehow, it's perfect. And there are lessons for my husband in all this as well, namely coming to terms with his fear-centric view of himself and the world, and where he thinks I fit into it. This is all about embracing love. I am out of resonance with his deep fear-based way of being, and I have said what I can to help him. I've asked him to see this as an opportunity, as a time of great faith, a time of being bold and jumping into the unknown.

He's afraid we'll lose the house, lose the brewery business and he'll have to live with his parents. He said he's afraid he'll die all by himself and no one will find him for days. (He really said this.) He is afraid he won't be able to handle the stress of starting a new business without me here "as his crutch". (He really said that, too.)

There are so many unknowns and no guarantee of safety. This is true. Though I've been assured by my guides that this is going to work out well for me *and* for my husband. Those in our etheric support system have our backs and will help things go smoothly.

I feel this also represents an opportunity for my husband to love me and support me unconditionally. I've learned in our 30-year relationship that if it impacts our money, and it's not something he values, it's not going to get his support. This happened as far back as the 1990s when I was paying for my Reiki attunements. It happened when I discovered craniosacral work 15 years ago and wanted to do training in California. It happened when I decided to enroll in massage school so I could get my license to practice craniosacral work. I'd say overall, he tolerated my spiritual interests. This is worlds away from feeling authentic, loving, enthusiastic support.

I moved forward with many of my interests and learnings anyway over the years. Granted, he took care of the kids when I was gone or in class, and after a while he settled into quiet acceptance during those few years of massage school. And he enjoyed the occasional massage and Reiki treatment. But I never heard any words of encouragement or support for the money and time it took for me to learn these skills, nor did he offer a touch of excitement for me moving into this line of work as a career.

When I finished massage school about ten years ago, my husband's work-related back pain and back problems were to a point of debilitation. This was not a good time for me to quit my job and move into the alternative healing space where I wouldn't be making enough money to support us. I made a conscious decision then to put my aspirations of going into healing work full-time on the back burner.

Looking back, I believe that my decisions to move forward with those things like Reiki and craniosacral work—where I found bliss, excitement, inspiration, and a deep connection to my spirit—prepared me for this pivotal moment. It's the same idea. I must move forward with this journey to Mexico even if my husband doesn't fully support it. I do recognize the stakes are higher this time around, there's more at stake for both of us.

Until last summer, several years had gone by with me being pretty disconnected from the spiritual side of myself—me being focused on the remodeling of our house, focused on my career and clients, focused on getting our youngest son through college. Then my world changed completely when I met my spirit guide, Micah, via a psychic in June 2018.

Micah and I developed a close relationship very quickly, once I officially "knew" about him. Micah gave me a big clue as to what was to come on July 8th, 2018, almost three months before Metatron came into my world. I was cleaning the house, sweeping I think, when this knowledge flowed in. I captured the gist of the message in my journal entry that day: "Okay! So, I heard you loud and clear—WOW. My life's purpose is to use my healing gift. My challenge is to dive into the work without regard to my personal financial well-being, and regardless of the needs, comfort and wishes of one person" (referring to my husband).

At the time I didn't know how this was going to play out, but it certainly resonated, given the past with my husband.

While I have many channeled messages from several sources supporting this life change, I still am experiencing fear. I just want to be as sure as possible this is the right move, and this is the right timing. This is one of the main things that Metatron told me has held me back in this lifetime—my need to always be "right". To do the "right" thing. To think and plan and research and over-think, think, think, think things to death to help ensure the best outcome possible. I just can't do that in this case. It's all about my heart and love.

I have already found the place I'll be renting in Baja, in a little town called Spa Buena Vista. That part was super easy! When I saw the rental listing online, my energy flared up. I pay attention when this happens! Just as Metatron described—it's only a single room, just enough space for me. Palapa roof. Very inexpensive, under $500 per month. Walking distance to the beach and town. It is perfect, and I've already made tentative arrangements with the landlord who is from Oregon which is not far from where I live now.

February 4, 2019

I asked to speak with Metatron directly this morning on this move and my mission and facing my fears. It was an incredible 20-minute channeling. He brought my energy vibration down deep and guided me to "go with the flow", to give over my fears to him and to take the final step.

Metatron, as recorded on my phone:

> *"Shawna, let the energy flow. Let your energy flow. Let the energy take you very, very deep. Let go of needing to spin your Merkaba. Let go of your fear of failure, of not doing this right, your fear of rejection. Your fear of not meeting Ramirah. There you go my child. Take a deep breath.*
>
> *"You are beauty manifest. Yes, a true angel of God. Our avatar, our mouthpiece, so brave. You are at the zero point. Release all fear. Release all need to be anything at all. Release all expectations of yourself. Release attachment to what this is supposed to feel like.*
>
> *"Let the wave take over. Sit at the bottom of the ocean and let the gentle swaying of the water move you. You're not fighting it. You're not forcing it. You're not influencing it. You're simply going with the flow. And you start to feel Mother Earth below you, beneath you, around you and within you. And you become one with the water. Become one with the earth. You become one with the love that emanates all around you, and you are that love. It's within you, it is you. Now that you've truly made this decision, go with the flow. Let go of attachments. Let go of your worry. And let this love be your guide.*
>
> *"Rule from a place of an open heart. Not just from within your vessel, but from within everywhere. And with this natural expanded awareness, the knowing will be there. There will be no worry here. From this place you can manifest anything. Put your heart's desires out there, make them known. Come from a place of love, not fear.*
>
> *"Know that you lie in the cradle of oneness of God, of love, as a newborn babe, without a care in the world. With only love, curiosity. A blank slate. Picture yourself as that baby laying in that cradle. The cradle being swayed gently by God. With the light of God shining upon you and shining into your heart, reflecting back that perfection that you are. Unlearn what you have learned. Be this baby. Let the bliss be your guide.*
>
> *"Hand your fears over to me. Let me take your fears. Whatever those fears may be, give them to me now, my dear one."*

As my physical tears flowed, I said out loud to Metatron: "I give my fears to Metatron. I relinquish all my fears to Metatron. I clear them out of my energy system. I'm rolling them out of my system, out of my energy field and giving them to Metatron right now. All my fears of rejection, of failure, of the unknown, my fear of lack of safety and lack of knowing and assurances of outcomes, I give that to Metatron now. I give my fear of what people might think and what they might say to Metatron right now. I give my fears of not having money. I give my fears of what my husband is fearing to Metatron now. I give all my fears of all those around me directing fear to me, to Metatron now. I give my fear of not passing the ring pass not to Metatron now. I give these fears to Metatron now so that he may emancipate these fears and replace them with light and love, confidence, trust, faith. An unconditional light. Hope."

I am on my divine path. I am important to the emancipation of humankind. I will move mountains. I am that beacon of light for those who seek it. I am the pillar of strength for others who need it.

The tears and the fears faded away, and Metatron continued:

> *"Make this happen, Shawna. Take the final step. Do it with happiness and joy. Be bold with your soul. Let the flow of energy become you. Be here every day. We are with you throughout this entire emancipation process. We all share in the oneness. We are one. Shawna, you will come to know this very soon. Not just a knowing but a feeling and a truth, deep within your soul. And it will be that thing that catapults you deep into your mission, deep into the knowing. Where time doesn't exist. Where your desires manifest in real-time. This will be your new reality beyond what you can even fathom right now in your mind. Trust. Trust. Trust.*
>
> *"You have answered the Clarion Call. Rejoice in that Shawna. You've done it, you're almost there. You are answering the Clarion Call right now. This is your time; this is your time to shine. Literally shine this light. No more veil. Just the truth. Know this deep in your heart. You are the light, you are the love, you are the beacon. We are just helping you to remember this and to put you in a state where you'll be able to have clarity, clearness. Putting you in a place that will truly help facilitate what you need to be doing.*
>
> *"Yes, we are proud of you. But this shouldn't make a difference and it doesn't make a difference, because you are not doing this for us, you are doing this for you... and your brothers and sisters. And you are doing it unconditionally without the need for recognition. Without any expectation of what may come back to you. You give of yourself unconditionally.*
>
> *"Be in the flow, Shawna. Be in the flow. I love you and I leave you in peace."*

Thank you, Metatron. I love you, too.

February 10, 2019

I am about ready to give my notice at work. Possibly even as early as tomorrow. Deep breath. Stillness.

My husband has come around and is now supporting me with this move. Thank you, God. He beautifully defended me and this decision to my dad and his girlfriend a few nights ago. They are very worried about me, worried about my husband and perplexed about this entire situation. While timing is not great, timing has never been great for me to follow my heart. Timing will always be challenging when you are doing something like this. There'll never be a good time in anyone else's eyes. Because my leaving is scary. It adds chaos. It's not safe. It's unexpected. It's extremely risky on many fronts. It's crazy.

Even so, both of our children were so sweet and gracious when I told them tonight that this is happening. I mentioned these plans back in October when my husband and I first made the trip to Los Barriles, so it wasn't a big surprise. My heart is bursting with pride and love for these two beautiful young men.

Now I just need the nerve to quit my job.

I am stepping off the hamster wheel for a bit. Going to find myself, get closer to my heart. Get very quiet and listen to what the universe wants to say and experience what it has to offer. What will life be like when I "go with the flow" as Metatron says? What does that type of life look like? I'm going to do (not do) what I can to find out.

I see this time away as me being able to be in my little cocoon, emerging six months later as a butterfly. After this I don't expect to be working in marketing or doing anything that doesn't make my heart sing. Come what may.

I surrender. I am your avatar. With my free will I give myself over to my higher self and to divine will. *I am the light, I am the love, I am the beacon.*

February 16, 2019

This morning during my meditation, I see John the Baptist meditating with me. It has been a while! I am so glad to see him. I have to contain my excitement as to not move out of this altered meditative state.

John is sitting full lotus position with his eyes closed, facing me. This vision started very similar as to the experience I had October. With two fingers, he brings his hand to his third eye, then out toward my third eye, then back to his third eye, back and forth several times. This seems to deepen the connection.

I begin to see us sitting in that same open meadow of golden grasses, a gentle warm breeze flowing around us. I take a few deep breaths and try to settle in. I start to look around. I look down and see that my belly is huge and round with child. I'm wearing muslin or linen clothing which is fully draped over me. I look up at John and his eyes are still closed, still deep in meditation. Wow, I'm pregnant! I assume this is after the miscarriage of John's and my baby in the river.

I see myself slowly laying down, with my belly protruding up to the sky. From a detached place above myself, I see my legs spread and I start to bear down. This baby is about to be born. There are figures that begin to surround me, a few people who are helping me give birth. I don't see them clearly. They are more like shadows.

Pretty quickly I see the baby slide out of me with a gush of blood and fluid, umbilical still connected inside me. I'm waiting for it to cry or make a noise. Someone hands the baby up to me and I take the little one into my arms as I lay flat on the ground. I rolled over a bit to get a better look at this little person. Oh, my goodness, I am so relieved that the baby is alive. And it's a boy! He then starts crying the sweetest, tiniest cry. I am overjoyed with love.

I look up and John hasn't moved. I get the sense this is not his baby. Possibly this is after John has died. I then see Jesus come up from behind me. I'm now sitting up with the baby in my arms. Jesus is glowing light, beaming love and comfort. He puts his hands on my shoulders and looks down upon us as if blessing us with his loving gaze. I'm left wondering, who's the father of this baby?

Two days ago, I put my notice in at work, booked a one-way ticket to San Jose del Cabo and reserved my lodgings for the first six weeks. Trying not to panic. I'll be on that plane in four short weeks. I'm actually SUPER EXCITED. Bring it!!!

February 17, 2019

I clearly connected with my mom last night! Amazing! About a week ago, I said a little prayer to my mom, telling her that I hoped she was good with my decision to go to the Sea of Cortez. I told her I missed her and I hoped she was doing great. Just then, I felt an energy pulse from above my head, then another, and then another. Three bursts in a row. Then nothing for a few seconds. Then again three short energy pulses in a row. I knew immediately this was mom making her presence known. So very exciting and life affirming.

Last night, I felt those three energy pulses come in as I was lying in bed reading. Then I hear my mom's voice coming from my heart region, "Shawna can you hear me?" Wow, yes, I could hear her loud and clear, in her voice. She sounded so happy, clear, strong. Vibrant. I did not record this because it happened so quickly, but she told me that I am going to love it there, absolutely that I made the right decision. She talked about all the planning and coordination that is going on. The creation and the love. What a relief to hear this from my mom. So grateful. I thanked her for being an amazing mom, filling me with strength and confidence. I gave her big virtual hugs and just snuggled into her. She told me she is doing great. That I've been there where she's at now many, many times, just that I've forgotten what it's like.

This morning during my meditation I sought to connect with Ramirah deeply. I have recorded a channeled twin flame meditation that I do several times a week and have been doing for several months now. Today Ramirah and I traveled in our shared Merkaba to his planet. He expertly "steered" us there and we gently came to rest on the surface while still in our Merkaba. I saw super shimmery golden sand and sand dunes as far as the eye could see. The sky was not very bright, almost gray in color. Possibly it was what we'd think of as early morning.

The sand seemed to be vibrating, as though it was made from tiny particles of gemstones that are a bit translucent in nature. I could see shimmery waves of light coming off the surface of the sand. So incredibly beautiful. I looked to my left and saw a large sun or possibly a planet reflecting light. It was huge on the horizon and hazy pink in color. It wasn't very bright, as though I was viewing it through a thick atmosphere. I didn't see any other beings or structures, just this vibrant sand. I asked Ramirah the name of his planet and I heard the word "Neptune". This caught me by total surprise. Hmmm. Not sure I heard that right, but the word did repeat a few times. I'll need to do some research on this. I think Neptune is a big gas planet to us. But I do believe that in other dimensions, these types of planets can be completely different and teaming with life not observable to us in the third dimension. Interesting!

February 23, 2019

March 18th, the day I will arrive in Baja. Only three short weeks away. I know I've made the right decision and am feeling more and more grounded in it.

My best friend for the past 20 years or so is having a very hard time with all this. Lots of fear. I'll refer to her as Monica. She told me she is very worried about me. She asked me how I can be doing this, not listening to my friends and family who are concerned for me. How can I be so selfish, she said. She hasn't had a lot of exposure to spiritual and other-worldly concepts such as these, and I'm pretty sure she thinks I've gone crazy. She's not only concerned about me, she's mad about it. She may be taking it personally. I opened up to her several months ago about some of what was happening with me, meeting my spirit guide, meeting Metatron, and it seemed to go over like a lead balloon. She is not sharing in my excitement one bit.

I try to think, how can I stay in my heart space here? How do I live this path of unconditional love? How do I speak my truth without sounding defensive? I want to honor where she's at in her journey, yet still honor myself. Mentally, physically, spiritually, emotionally—what is the best course of action for everyone involved?

Metatron and the Galactic Council said many times in their books that we cannot be worried about what other people are going to think and say about our transformations and our journeys. It's easy to understand this, but harder to put it into practice I'm finding. I am struggling with this. I'm trying to be empathizing and understanding instead of feeling abandoned and rejected.

February 24, 2019

A loving exchange with Ramirah tonight!!! AMAZING. AFFIRMING. I need affirming right now!

Me: Ramirah, it has been way too long since I wrote you. My apologies. But I am sure you have felt me reaching out to you with all my beingness. Everything is in motion. I am so very excited to finally know, experience whatever it is that the Great Creator has in store for us. I will try to stay detached from specific outcomes and expectations for how this might unfold. Yet I stay focused on you and focused on our love and on our mission.

How are you my love? Are you there?

Ramirah: My darling surrender to us. Surrender to this. This is all that is left to do, all that is left to know. The universe watches over us carefully and will guide our lights until they merge as one. We only have to allow it. Completely surrender, and yes, detach. Oh, the glory for our union. My dear this will be amazing and inspiring. Do not worry yourself any longer about this. All decisions have been made and plans are in motion.

Me: Thank you Ramirah!

Ramirah: Thank you my darling for all the sacrifices you are making and have made. Bold and brave. Soon. We are so close. I can't wait to hold you, smell you, devour you with my energy until the separation between us is completely gone. A pure absorption into oneness. Where anything is possible. You just need surrender.

February 28, 2019

Feeling such peace and gratitude this morning. The sun has just popped up above the horizon flooding my living room with golden sunshine. I'm feeling light, my lungs feeling more expansive, my head feeling clear.

Tonight, Monica and I are meeting for dinner. My plan is to bring all the love and understanding I can muster, total acceptance and empathy.

The messages and channelings have become pretty quiet since I fully committed to this move. This is a time for me to focus on preparing, getting all my business in order. Continuing to work through emotions and fears with my husband, my dad. I'd like to leave for the airport with absolutely no worries and minimal lose ends. I don't want to bring any extra baggage with me.

I keep hearing/feeling the message that "*my inner life will become more important than my outer life*". Usually this message is accompanied with a bit of vibration or energy shift.

March 4, 2019

Well, the dinner with Monica was a complete fiasco. Huge test for me in unconditional love and non-judgment. I am struggling. I am wondering how my best friend of over 20 years could turn on me like this and treat me this way.

She called me crazy, among other things. She said it feels like I've died… like this is a death for her. Me talking to angels, spirit guides and "aliens and crazy shit" …me taking off by myself to Mexico. She just can't relate to any of it, can't understand it. She said we don't have anything in common now. She can no longer be my friend. It's just too much for her. She's unapologetic. I did the best I could to try to salvage the friendship using love and encouragement. Thirty minutes into the meal, she put on her coat and the waitress boxed up our uneaten food to go.

Monica has also been going through her own personal pain now for months. Physical issues, mental and emotional stress and strain. She's told me previously that what I'm doing has caused her stress which makes her symptoms worse. I've asked about this and she doesn't want to share anything with me. My understanding is that this ascension process is helping to bring all our issues to the surface where they must be dealt with. This is likely a big factor.

She did text me Friday and tried to offer more context around her feelings and how she treated me at dinner. She said she is truly heartbroken that our "connection is somewhat broken", due to what I am "becoming". She said she has built a wall around her heart to protect herself. She did say that she wishes me happiness on my journey and she'll miss me. This was a nice change of tone and a rare opening-up for her. It gave me some hope that she wasn't ready to completely write me off.

On Saturday March 2nd I participated via Skype in Robbie Mackenzie's NYC Meditation Meetup group where he channeled Metatron. I had been up at 4 a.m. that morning thinking about Monica and all the things I wanted to say to her. Mostly defensive. But I knew I needed to wait until after this meditation, after any messages from Metatron before I did that. I'm so glad I waited.

Robbie started his channeling, and it was as if Metatron was speaking directly to me about this situation. Metatron's initial words, via Robbie:

> *"There are many of you who are transforming, all over your globe. Many coming out of their cosmic egg and being birthed into a higher consciousness. You're supporting this vibration as you pray, as you meditate, as you stay in your center, as you do not judge anybody or anything within this transformation. For there are many who appear to be stuck in their duality. But they are ready to come out of their cosmic egg.*
>
> *"There are many being squeezed tightly by the circumstances you as a collective have created in your globe. Your circumstances of pressure. You don't judge anything. You don't judge anybody. Everything is happening in perfect divine timing. The cosmic egg is cracking. Divine love is expanding. Your light is shining. You are in the perfect place at the perfect time. Do not concentrate on doing, concentrate on being."*

This hit me square in my heart center and I realized this truly is a test for me, to put into action all the love I've been practicing these past six months. To show Monica as much love and compassion that I can, absolutely no judgment for her, only love. I told her right then in a text that I love her unconditionally and I'll always have room for her in my heart no matter what. I felt a lightness come over me and sensed it probably did for her as well. Love with no attachment and no expectations. Be this every day.

Truly embodying only love, no fear, no judgment… I am grateful for this test and have felt myself shift into a more expansive awareness these past two days. This is my mission. I'm doing it now. Feeling complete joy, gratitude and peace. I am humbled.

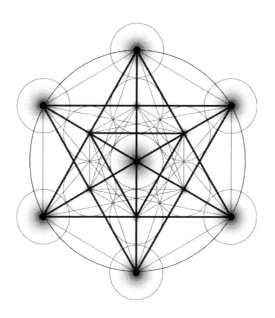

PART TWO:
OPEN & EXPAND

This is all about experiencing duality for the one infinite creator. People often ask, why do we lose our memory of who we are when we are born? It's because you are all God, and if you remembered that you were God, you wouldn't be able to have this horrible experience.

- Corey Goode, *Ascension & End Times Prophecy*
Corey Goode at Cosmic Waves - Part 1, online video

March 18, 2019

WELL GANG?!?

I'm on the plane. Heading to SJD. WTF?!

Hard to believe I've finally made it this far. THANK YOU, Metatron, Galactic Council. For all your love and guidance, energy downloads, helping me to prepare. Thank you, HUBBY! I love you so much. Your support is making this possible.

Thank you, my wonderful sons! Thank you, Dad! Thank you, Mom. Thank you, my brother and sister. I love you all so much.

"Emancipate Reptilian energy." Okay! I am ready! I am honored to serve.

Oneness. Bliss. Ascension. Love.

Ancient. Sacred. Mystical.

Focus with detachment.

Today's song stuck in my head: REO Speedwagon—*I Believe It's Time for Me to Fly*

March 19, 2019

I am LOVING it here. My little round one-room casita, "the yurt", is perfect. So amazing to be sitting here on this bed after seeing pictures of it for so many weeks. It's even better than I had imagined. I spent almost an hour in the hot spring-fed outdoor tub last night. Watched the sky darken and the moon brighten. Watched Orion come into view, watched all the stars pop out. Prayed to the moon for protection on this journey. Opened my heart to the moon and sent it love. Felt the light reflecting from its surface fill up my third eye.

Two days leading up to this journey, I felt my energy revving up… sweet waves of blissful full-body vibrations for maybe ten minutes at a time. Sitting on the plane after it landed at SJD, more waves of beautiful energy. On the ride out to the yurt, a blanket of peace washed over me. I feel this extra energy as the presence of Metatron letting me know he's with me and we are beginning. The raising of the vibration is starting.

Meditating this morning sitting on my double bed, I was barely into the meditation sequence and the tears started to flow. The lesson was "softness". I can be softer. The balancing out of my soft feminine side along with my more masculine side. It's okay to be soft. This will be my focus for now. I don't need to be so hard. I felt like I had to be hard and strong to get here to Mexico, to deal with the fear and negativity coming my way. Now that I'm here, I can put down that armor and be soft.

I definitely feel my energy amplified here in this environment. I AM LOVING THIS. I AM LOVE. Spread it!

March 20, 2019

Last night as I drifted off to sleep, I envisioned a young man with long dark wavy hair showing me a three-dimensional triangle and a round sphere. He showed each to me, held them up. Then the triangle doubled to make the shape of a Merkaba. He placed the double pyramid into the middle of the circle/sphere. He smiled at me and lifted his eyebrows, as if to say, *do you get this?* I got it. Picture my Merkaba in the middle of a globe. He told me that we'll be working on this during my dream state, and that I shouldn't try to remember my dreams for now.

Yesterday was a beautiful, surreal whirlwind. Up at dawn, watched the sunrise from the beach, ate a hearty breakfast, meditated, took off for the beach with my bathing suit on. After soaking up some sunshine on the beach for an hour, my inner voice told me it was time to go into town. I gathered up my stuff and started walking toward the road. Lo and behold, there was the landlord with a car full of folks, coming to find me and to pick me up! He had mentioned the first day that they'd be going to town but hadn't told me a time. I hope my intuition expands now that my mind isn't occupied with thoughts of work.

This is how I want to be every minute of every day while I'm down here—let my higher self, my inner guidance, show me the way. Get out of my own way and let divine will take over. For everything. When to wake up, when to get out of bed, when to eat, what to eat. When to meditate, how to meditate. When to read, what to read. Every decision, I will go with the flow. Be in the flow. If a thought crosses my mind that needs action, I'll do it. I will be conscious. This is also what the Galactic Council had said several weeks ago—that now is the time for me to start following my higher self.

The yurt landlords have been so welcoming and supportive. They happen to be here as well, on vacation. They own the home that sits behind this property. I feel their unconditional love and acceptance. Their friends who are visiting now are beautiful people, too. I am blessed. They hosted a big dinner at their place with nine of us. Lots of laughing and interesting conversations about driving down Baja to Spa Buena Vista all the way from Oregon. Many of them have done that drive more than once and never had any problems. They never felt scared or threatened.

It's interesting being here by myself. I wonder if this will be more the norm—people like the landlords and their friends "taking me in" and including me because I'm here by myself. Seems that if my husband or family was with me, there'd be more distance and space. It makes for a very different travel experience.

Everyone back home has been so sweet. Loving my pictures and wishing me the best. My husband especially.

I've started reading a new book, *The Archangel Guide to Enlightenment and Mastery: Living in the Fifth Dimension,* by Diana Cooper and Tim Whild.[8] This information also happens to be related to or influenced by Archangel Metatron, per the author. I had no idea when I purchased it! No doubt in my mind that this book was specifically dropped into my awareness at just the right time. A whole new set of meditations and visualizations to take my ascension to the next level. Thank you, Metatron.

I can't help but wonder about coming together with Ramirah and the potential for extraordinary love and bliss when it happens. Mind-blowing concept. I surrender to my higher self.

My husband does not know about Ramirah.

March 21, 2019

Such a great day! So affirming! I am humbled by this process.

There are four yurts on this lot. The one next door to me is being rented by a 73-year-old woman from Vancouver, Canada. I will call her Grace. She's here looking for some self-healing for her soul and for various health issues. She has always been into alternative care and spiritual practices like Tai Chi and Yoga. She has been keenly interested in my journey and my story and we've spent some time getting to know each other these past few days. She's strong and sweet and ready to get better. She is also by herself. Go girl!

As mentioned, I'm going with the flow and letting my higher self guide me. Today I had the thought that I should offer to help Grace with energy work and ask her if she'd like to meditate with me. As she walked past my yurt to head to the beach, I made the offer. She seemed very excited to give me a try. I told her that I'd look into a meditation that we could do together this afternoon.

She went on her way and I retreated back into my yurt. I brought with me a beautiful pendant that my dad gave me the day before I left for Mexico—it represents Metatron with a gold merkaba dotted by the seven chakras, set on a lavender fluorite stone. I place the pendant in my palm and ask for Metatron's support and guidance whenever I wear it. The pendant hangs from a gold chain which I placed around my neck. I then asked for help in channeling a meaningful meditation for Grace. I asked for help from Metatron, my higher self, Grace's spirit guides and any other loving beings who'd like to contribute. I asked for protection for this process.

I took a few deep breaths and felt my energy and consciousness fall into a bit of a trance state. I pressed the record button on my laptop and started channeling a meditation custom-made for Grace. All the words and imagery flowed easily. There were times when I was in awe of this process and how the visuals and messages came forth in a natural way. Around 22 minutes into this flow, the meditation came to a close. I was feeling pretty excited about it.

Later this afternoon Grace came over to my yurt to do the meditation together. We spent a good 20 minutes talking further about our situations and exchanging ideas on spiritual topics. We then sat facing each other on my white resin chairs and listened to the speaker on my laptop play my recording. I felt the meditation very strongly. Lots of energy flowing between the two of us. I was aware of not only my own process as the meditation progressed, but also hers. I could sense sadness at times, a closed throat chakra. I did my best to follow along, yet also hold space for her process.

When it was finished, Grace opened her eyes slowly. She said she was full of disbelief in how spot-on it was, how perfect it was for her situation. She was genuinely surprised and said there was no doubt that I had the help of higher guidance. She said it was 100% accurate for her. I am so honored to be of service in this way, delighted that she found meaning in it. She told me she wants to do the meditation every day.

Within the next few days we'll try some bodywork, too. Exciting! The healing and channeling for others has already started, just like the Galactic Council and Metatron said I'd be doing here.

Tonight after dinner I read Lee Carroll's latest Kryon channeling from February 2019 that speaks specifically to healers about the changing nature of what we do. Kryon said, "A full-body healing doesn't mean just all the organs and the mental processes, it means dealing with perceptions of the past."[7] Dealing with the PERCEPTIONS of the past. It's not even really about *what* happened to you or what you may have experienced, it's about *how* you perceived it and what residual illusory imaginings you have chosen to keep in your beingness.

Plus, we just don't hold that imagining in our minds—it's in our four-body system because all are linked—physical, mental, emotional and spiritual. This is why stress can so easily create dis-ease in the body. Everything is one grand ecosystem. Stagnant energy breeds physical ailments. Lack of physical movement breeds stagnant energy. Everything needs to stay in motion and moving forward, evolving—that movement generates its own momentum and keeps the energy flowing.

I am reminded that true healing comes when people feel *deeply seen* and *deeply heard*. I learned this from Hugh Milne, of the Visionary Craniosacral Work ® LLC Milne Institute, during my time many years ago learning craniosacral therapy from him in California. All the meditations and body work are great tools, but lasting healing comes when you are able to connect at a deep level with the person with whom you're working. At our core, each of us yearn for this.

March 24, 2019

Being here in Baja has been awesome. I am loving it. Sunshine, sunrises, sunsets…full moons… clear turquoise ocean water, snorkeling…super nice people, an opportunity to completely let go and relax. Take it moment by moment. I am still pinching myself.

The Galactic Council came through yesterday morning after my Merkaba meditation, telling me to double up on protection. I felt the telltale sign of tension in my throat and jaw, accompanied by subtle waves of energy. I asked if anyone wanted to come through with a message. I recorded this on my phone.

"Hi Shawna. Such strength, beauty and grace. I know that makes you uncomfortable for you to hear this now, but it is absolutely the truth of who you are at your core."

(Thank you, thank you so much.)

"Please listen to me carefully. The time to ask for protection is now. Picture yourself enveloped in white protective light that is impenetrable from outside evil forces. We've been maintaining this light for you for some time now. It's coming up to the point where we need to double up on this energy field, this protection for you, because things are going to be shifting pretty rapidly. Ask Ra for protection. Ask Metatron for protection. Call upon the Galactic Council and our armies of light to surround you at all times, to be in your energy space, in your field permanently. When you wake up in the morning, ask for protection and picture this white light, the energy, all these beings, in your energy field focused on you, deflecting and reflecting out anything negative that may be coming your way. Do it again in the middle of the day, the same thing. And then again before you go to bed.

"This vibration that you are walking into, that you will be embodying will be a beacon—not only a beacon for others who are seeking enlightenment and healing and love and joy, and who are on this similar path as you—it will also be a beacon for negative energy. The Cabal. Those who are seeking to squash and extinguish the fires that are burning so bright. They are looking for people like you for energies that you have and embody. They're going to do what they can to extinguish those flames. So, let's double up, ask for protection, breathe in this protective white light. Several times a day. We'll continue to do our part as well as we have been.

"Once you do that, you can surrender. We don't want you to be in fear over this extra protection. Everything will happen just as it should. Everything will unfold for you just as it should—at the right time, at the right place, in the right way. So, once the protection in is there and you've invoked it, you don't have to think about it again.

"We are so honored to be working with you, Shawna. So excited for the next phase of your journey. You are doing wonderfully. That light is shining. That vibration is going out to the universe. You are making a difference."

(I also asked about Ramirah. They told me that Ramirah is already here. ALREADY HERE. I started crying.)

"Ramirah is already here. Oh, my child, soon. Your energies will merge as one. Oh, the joy and the wonder. We are in awe for both of you, for the energy you're going to create together and all the good it will do. All in good time, just as it's supposed to. Such a beautiful, divine coupling. It's well-deserved Shawna, well-deserved. I leave you with all the peace, all the love, all the happiness you deserve, Shawna. Don't forget your protection."

March 26, 2019

I continue to read Diana Cooper's book, *The Archangel Guide to Enlightenment and Mastery*. Enjoying it immensely. I am anchoring in key concepts that resonate and help me have a broader understanding of what is going on right now. She explains that a master can keep a high vibration in a physical body, no matter what is happening in your life. You just float above and ride the wave like a pro.

This summarizes in very simple terms what I'm striving to do, what I'm being directed to do and what the book *Metatron - This is The Clarion Call: All You Need to Know* explained. It's helpful to get the slightly different perspective that is coming through Diana in this case.

Metatron, in the *Clarion Call* book, has also described a major test and initiation as part of soul's evolution and eventuality of experiencing oneness with everything—passing the "ring pass not". Metatron explains that there will come a major test in our individual ascension process of our ability to embody love and not fear. If we are able to embody love in any situation, even the most frightful of events, we pass the ring pass not and our Merkabas open up.[6] HUGE part of this ascension process. It hasn't happened to me yet, though I feel that I'm being trained through various dreams and nightmares these past six months. I haven't been doing very well! But more and more I am at least able to wake up and understand the lesson being presented and what I could have done differently to not be in fear but instead be in love.

Diana also talks about the Merkaba. At a certain point, she says, after your feminine and masculine sides become balanced, the Merkaba becomes a ball, a circular shape that "can hold more light".[8] I love this concept.

I believe this is the same idea that the young man with the long dark hair was showing me a few nights ago—the Merkaba inside this ball. When I do my Merkaba meditation now, I sense my upper chakras above my crown chakra engaged, and I see this all happening inside a globe. And since I've started asking for protection four times a day, I see all of *that* within my bubble of protection. I've been picturing this protection bubble with a mirrored surface that reflects and deflects anything negative. My state of consciousness goes very deep with this request for protection and the visualization of this impenetrable reflective ball of white loving light. I feel this love and protection deeply.

This is another very important part of the greater ascension process underway right now. Diana writes that "a master radiates an open heart, and this allows one with a closed heart to see the reflection of who they truly are."[8]

Also related to the challenging times we find ourselves in today, Diana writes:

> The initial phase of the ascension energy has now been integrated into the planet… As the frequency of our planet rises, every sentient being is affected by it, including humans… Once this transformation starts to occur, the fifth-dimensional heart begins to illuminate and decisions are heart centered. Now this soul presents the

person with tests to ensure that their heart is fully in command. This is one reason why people are receiving so many challenges right now. It is a sign that they are ready to move to the next phase, as tough paths indicate high callings.[8]

I love that! *Tough paths indicate high callings.*

Diana has a lot to say about physically moving to another location to help carry out your mission, which is exactly what I've been called to do. She believes that our spirit knows exactly where we are supposed to be on the planet.[8]

She says that when you are unified with your chosen spot, your personal energy will rise dramatically. This aligns with what Metatron and the Galactic Council have been telling me. Moving here to the Sea of Cortez will allow me to step fully into my mission which will include massively raising my vibration. HOW COOL IS THAT!?! HOW AWESOME IS SPA BUENA VISTA AND THE SEA OF CORTEZ!?! Truly my heaven on Earth right now.

To wrap up this idea, Diana also talks about the importance of these journeys some of us are taking. We are anchoring the light at specific places as part of a global grid.

According to Diana's book, our current ascension plan is based on how the people of Atlantis used to live and thrive 260,000 years ago. This "template" will be applied to Earth after the current transition is complete, around 2032 according to her book. Soul groups that were alive and ascended during the golden time of Atlantis have agreed to reincarnate at this particular time to help with this current ascension. Because of this, our ascension event has created great interest in the rest of the galaxy and many advanced beings are anticipating with excitement our unfolding. She says these beings are not only witnessing this evolution, but they are helping in their "special and unique manner."[8] I have definitely experienced this firsthand with my relationship with Roykilva and other non-earth-human entities. Metatron has communicated through me and others that this ascension is being watched closely and is supported by millions of other non-Earth entities.

I had an amazing Merkaba meditation this morning. Spent extra time in the triad with John the Baptist (who I haven't seen in a while) and Jesus—joined in hands to make a triangle and sending a white column of love light straight up to the Christ grid. So deep and beautiful. The depth of my consciousness keeps expanding and evolving with every day that I'm here.

Yesterday Grace let me do some craniosacral with her, a bit of massage and more energy work. So fun! We are working on opening her heart a bit and her being patient and gentle with herself as she works on her healing. Goddess warrior.

Today Metatron said to me "*Anything you want.*" I was making a salad for lunch. This stopped me. Then a subtle sweet wave of loving energy washed over me. He was saying I can have anything I want, manifest anything. There are no limits. He's there, supporting me. Such love. Sigh.

I reached out to Monica with a text to see how she's doing. We exchanged some pleasantries.

March 28, 2019

I know I sound like a complete broken record, BUT these past two days have been amazing!

I was feeling a bit sad tonight, longing to meet Ramirah and wondering when and how that was going to happen. And IF it was going to happen. I sent him love from my heart chakra and re-read the letter exchange we had on Feb. 23rd. So sweet. It made me feel so much better. I started to write him another letter tonight when suddenly my heart lit up with the most loving and nurturing energy. It just washed over my body and made me buzz with light. That is all the affirmation I need that this will all happen just as it should. I will not worry and wonder about it any longer, just trust and send him love.

As I smiled and put my hands on my heart, soaking in this bliss, an image started to form in my mind of me getting crowned or having a crown on my head. This is a somewhat familiar vision. I saw this during the time of John the Baptist, and I've seen it while envisioning myself on Ramirah's planet. I got the sense that Ramirah and I were a high priest and high priestess in Atlantis. I could see Ramirah as the man that Sharon described with a recent psychic reading— dark hair, muscular, turquoise eyes. He and I were together as lovers in Atlantis. I then had the vision of both Ramirah and I having matching clear crystal skulls placed into our throat chakras. The message I received was that these skulls have all the knowledge we need to carry out our mission and that information will be released as we need it. This reminded me of the reading I had with Elaine on Nov. 30. When Elaine told me that I was a high priestess in Atlantis, my energy went nuts. I'll file away this vision for a later time.

Yesterday I felt the urge to reach out to the "The Source" entities. I had connected with them first last October when I visited Los Barriles. Since then I have connected with them three additional times. They told me they are from the 10th dimension. Just about every time I've connected with them, I cry. Basking in their massive, loving presence is emotionally overwhelming. They feel absolutely huge and all-knowing. It's mind-blowing! I have such reverence for them.

The first three times I connected with them, I envisioned myself in a fish-tank type environment. Clear cube container, me floating peacefully in water, gravel beneath me, a light illuminating me. They told me that this was necessary so I would be comfortable, since our levels of vibration were so far apart.

This last time, yesterday, was different. My frequency has changed and also, they seemed to be helping raise my vibration even higher. Their messages for me were truly life changing. When I want to make this connection, I reach out to Heru and I do two meditations from Heru as described in the Return of Light teachings[9]—the one where you say "He" (hay) with your in-breath in your mind as you picture a cord going up as high from your crown as you can imagine, then "Ru" as you breathe out, picturing that cord going as far below you as possible. Did this for about five minutes. Followed with the meditation where you go into your heart over and over. I did this for a few minutes. Then I pictured myself between two pyramids where the light shines, which accesses this portal to these entities. I assume these are Egyptian pyramids given this involves Heru.

I connected and felt I was sitting upright, instead of laying down floating in a tank. I immediately felt tension deep in my throat, behind my sinuses. Then the tears start flowing. I knew the connection was made when the tears started. I was also feeling an itch and a pressure on the back of my head, on the outside of my head. That was bizarre.

Given the tension and pressure, I asked if they were there and if they could hear me. The Source replied immediately.

The Source: Yes, we are here and we are so glad to welcome you into our space again.

Me: Thank you so much. You are making my heart burst. And I feel your love and I feel pride—for what I'm doing and for what we are doing together. I feel that pride and love reflected back to me.

Is today the day that I come together with my twin flame? Can you tell me anything?

The Source: Your shift does seem imminent. You are on the precipice.

(At that point I see myself at the edge of a huge waterfall, leaning over it, then tumbling over with complete surrender. No fear. I see myself going over the waterfall a couple times, and it's delightful. I continue to feel this deep, deep tension in my head. I feel my vibration speeding up. Buzzing. My energy is moving. I get the sense they are raising my vibration in real time as we are connected. I said out loud that my frequency seemed to be picking up speed. I asked if they were helping to raise my vibration.)

The Source: Actually, my dear one, your vibration is higher. You are resonating with our energies in a different way. Your energy coming together with our energy is causing a resonance here. It is so exciting to witness this.

(This was very exciting for me as well. I happen to be sitting on the couch in my yurt instead of the bed, where I had my feet firmly planted on the cement floor. Great for grounding. I sat there for several minutes, letting this energy come in, flow out my crown. Soaking it in. The tension deep in my head got even stronger. It felt like I was breathing as one with the universe. The Source told me we were making this happen together.)

Ahead of this connection, I prepared a few questions that I wanted to ask them, mostly about the ascension. When I came to the point where I was going to ask them, it become obvious that the questions were completely meaningless. The questions involve either the past or the future, neither of which exist. Only the present moment is real. The message that flowed quietly and slowly from my mouth, unified as one with The Source.

The Source & Me, As One: There is only right now. Questions involve the future or the past which don't exist. LET GO OF ALL QUESTIONS. Let go of all fears. There is only this present moment. For absolute faith and trust—the only way you can be… in this present moment.

The Source: Drop all your questions. Join us. Right now.

Embody love. Beam that love out. It's the only thing that exists.

Live in this moment, Shawna. Integrate and resonate. In this way, you are God. In this moment, you are God. Dissolve your ego. Become one with all that is.

Have complete trust and faith. Only love, no fear.

As I sat there, fully connected with this peace, I see how this peace is going to radiate out for others. Others' energy fields will start to get in alignment with my energy field. It will feel like they are flying, weightless; binds broken, they will feel unlocked. They will spread their wings and be free. Freedom. This is about freedom. Freedom from fear and illusion.

The experience was beautiful. Absolute stillness. I felt out of my body. The connection lasted about 22 minutes.

All questions are fear-based. In the one infinite moment, there are no questions. Only being.

March 30, 2019

Last night Grace and I met up with the landlords and their friends for dinner again. As we sat in the living room before taking off to the restaurant, I physically felt my energy open up and relax and my heart space radiate out love to the group. I wasn't even aware I was energetically holding myself "close to the chest" like that until it released. What a freeing, expanded feeling that was. So much easier and more natural. I will strive to be conscious of this "holding" and "releasing" all the time.

Dinner was fabulous and the conversations were interesting. One of the men in attendance said he was curious about my situation and wondered how it came to be that my husband supports me being here. He was asking with complete respect and genuineness. These are very smart, liberal men, but this concept—of me being here by myself—may be a bit hard to swallow. Each of them do have extremely smart, independent, successful women as wives, and I do feel their support for my journey and genuine curiosity for what I'm doing. I told the group that my husband's acceptance had been quite a process, that we had both learned and grown through that process. In terms of the ascension and things like aliens and archangels, I am not ready to talk about that during a casual group dinner.

I am feeling the restorative power of this place. The water, sun, wind, sand, stars; birds, lizards, bees. Beautiful people. The natural hot spring thermal waters. I am sinking into this world more and more every day. Asking for protection four times a day. Connecting deeply with that vision of impenetrable loving light protection. I am humbled.

April 1, 2019

Tomorrow—two weeks here already. Ramirah. Ramirah. RAMIRAH.

The end of March came and went. I have to remind myself that ALL IS PERFECT. ALL IN ITS RIGHT TIME.

FAITH. TRUST. LOVE.

Continue to be in my mission; raising my vibration by meditating; radiating out white love light; being the beacon for those who seek it, the strength for those who need it. Every time. Every person. Every situation. NO FEAR. Only love.

See the illusion for what it is. Follow my bliss. Be in the now. Go with the flow. All is one.

I have been re-reading the introduction to *RA: The Law of One - Book 1 The Ra Material.* The central concepts are as important and as relevant as ever. More so now that we are possibly getting closer to the cosmic unveiling of a new Earth.

The Law of One introduction helps explain why extraterrestrials and other evolved beings outside Earth use telepathy and channeling as their primary means of contact. They also say that meditation is the key to making this contact.

The authors of the book quote an entity by the name of Hatonn, from the Confederation of Planets. Hatonn gives a reason why telepathy is the preferred method of contact versus widespread, concrete proof of UFOs and extraterrestrials:

> We offer them no concrete proof, as they have a way of expressing it. We offer them Truth. This is an important function of our mission—to offer Truth without proof. In this way, the motivation will, in each and every case, come from within the individual. In this way, the individual vibratory rate will be increased. An offering of proof or an impressing of this Truth upon an individual in such a way that he would be forced to accept it would have no usable effect upon his vibratory rate.
>
> This, then, my friends, is the mystery of our way of approaching your peoples. [9]

Hatonn also talks about the importance of free will and not forcing a belief in any of these concepts, which must be evaluated from within:

> We find it necessary to give to those who seek that which they seek in such a way that they, for themselves, may appraise its value and accept or reject, on their own terms, those thoughts that we bring, and understand the reality of the creation in which all of us exist. [9]

The authors state that the basic core messages are consistent across all the channelings they did over those decades. Many of these coincide with the channelings I've done and the messages I've received. These include:

- The planet is going through a major vibratory shift. This shift will bring devastation and death but will also usher in a beautiful rebirth—Earth's Golden Age. The time draws near, but exact timing is unknown.

- We as humans are being given a choice as this time draws near—choose love, or not. It won't be enough to state verbally that your choice is love, you must embody love with your actions, thoughts and words. Your choice impacts what happens to you at this time.

- We are all one, here to express ourselves as an individuated aspect of the Great Creator. The separation we perceive here on Earth is an illusion. While the illusion is here to help us grow and evolve, it's time to see beyond this illusion and to experience the oneness with all.

- Evolved beings and entities, including those not of this earth, are here to help us through this transition—to help those who are seeking information, understanding.

- Use meditation to experience this oneness; to know love, peace and joy; to receive messages from other-dimensional beings and to evolve your spirit.

- The core of who we are is love. Love is everything.

April 4, 2019

Grace, my Baja yurt neighbor, left for home yesterday. We'll be life-long friends. What a gift to have her join me at the beginning of this adventure. She seemed to embody the wisdom and insight that my mom would have provided. No doubt our souls go way back. What an honor to have been able to share these past two weeks with her.

Watching the stars at night. So incredibly beautiful out here when the sky is black and the air is calm. Millions of pinpoints of light. I have seen a few very interesting moving lights, particularly above Orion. Two lights moving in unison for a short distance—these did not continue through the sky like a satellite does. Flashing lights that don't seem to be moving like an airplane. And of course, a few shooting stars. I'm ready—beam me up, Scotty!

With Grace gone my time here will move into its next phase. I plan to go deeper and get quieter as the days go by. Re-reading my journal from late September and October when the messages about Ramirah and moving to the Sea of Cortez were first spoken.

From my hand-written journal on September 16th, 2018. I had connected strongly with Archangel Metatron, feeling a bit scared and unsure about everything that was happening. This is what he said to help prepare me for the major life changes I had coming.

> *"Your time of doubt will be coming to an end very soon. We have a team working on you and with you right now as you are well aware, and we are making great progress. You are critical to the future of mankind. I know this sounds daunting, and maybe it is, but know you have a literal army beside you, with you, in and around you, ready to heed your call. Ready to do your bidding. You are never alone."*

Metatron, his team and the Galactic Council spent a ton of time and effort working on me last year—all four parts of my beingness (mental, emotional, spiritual, physical). I am so humbled. It was around Labor Day last year (early September 2018) that I came into contact with the book brought forth by Archangel Metatron, channeled by Robbie Mackenzie called *Metatron - This is the Clarion Call: All You Need to Know.* This book completely changed my life and put me on the path I'm on today.

From the very first page of this book, my energy WENT CRAZY. Blissful, pulsing waves of energy flowing through my body, keeping me in this state of euphoria. I knew immediately that this was the truth, this stuff was real, this was meant for me. The words were mind blowing. Amazing, crazy, WTF messages accompanied by this energy vibration. What the hell is going on here!?! Aliens? Spaceships? Ascension of Mother Earth? Ascended Masters and Archangels? My mission? And the urgency of it all?

Tonight—felt a subtle energy rush and pictured Ramirah saying to me, "Don't be afraid of me. Feel into my energy." These energy rushes have been few and far between for months now. So, when it happens, it gets my attention.

Also, today the song stuck in my head: *Let 'Em In* by Wings (Paul McCartney). Someone may be knocking on my door soon, and I better let 'em in!

April 5, 2019

Okay—I actually dreamt that someone was knocking on my door last night. It woke me up. I threw on my nightgown and opened the door slowly. No fear! Stepped outside. Nothing except the beautiful star-filled night sky. I came back in and went back to bed. That was 3:30 am. I also dreamt this morning that a spaceship was hovering over me. Round disk and in the center on the bottom of the disk were several rings of round blue lights. When the blue lights were centered above me, I felt a subtle energy rush. This woke me up, too.

Mostly I am not remembering my dreams. When I do remember them, they seem to be from the early morning. I'm really dead tired by about 8:30 pm, lights out around 9 pm. Up before dawn usually, around 5:45 am. If I'm feeling up to it, I trot down to the beach and watch the sunrise and take a walk. WHICH IS TOTALLY WORTH IT. The sunrises make me cry.

Last night and this morning, felt a couple more energy blasts, from deep in my core. Something is definitely stirring. I'm trying not to get too overly excited. How the hell is this going to happen? Is Ramirah going to literally knock on my door as a physical being, in his Reptilian majesty? Or will this be only energetic? Or will he be occupying a human's body?

In any case, this is completely awesome and exciting. An experience so sacred, so deep, to come together with your twin flame. I picture Ramirah as a tall Reptilian humanoid—body similar to ours. Standing upright on two legs, a torso, arms, neck, head, but with dark green scales on most of his body. Except for his chest and stomach which are lighter. I see his hands with four fingers with sharp claws. His neck and shoulders are broad. His face contains deep wisdom and strength. Slightly elongated jaw, tiny sharp teeth, a long pink forked tongue. Raised arches above his orangeish eyes that have vertical pupils. Touches of yellow scales on his forehead. A raised and spiny ridge down the back of his neck, all the way down his large tail. Shorter but strong legs. Sharp nails on his toes.

I often picture him placing the left side of my neck in his mouth, as though he's biting my neck, but it is deeply euphoric and sexual—his teeth not piercing my skin but instead hitting very fine nerve endings on my neck, giving me shuddering bliss. It has a bit of a possessive feel to it, me completely surrendering to him and he claiming me as his own.

April 11, 2019

Beautiful morning here today. Went on a 5-mile hike with the landlord through the surrounding desert mountains. All in walking distance of my yurt. He has a massive appreciation for this area and knows it all like the back of his hand. We walked along the ridge of a nearby mountain range then dropped down into a canyon. Saw a Road Runner bird and a Tarantula Hawk bug. Large old cacti and other desert plants and trees. Crystal rocks mixed in with granite rocks and boulders. Truly beautiful scenery on the trail and across the vista to the Sea of Cortez.

Our conversation flowed effortlessly and was full of laughter and gentle teasing. I have no doubt in my mind that he and I are connecting here in Spa Buena Vista for a reason, and that the people I'm meeting here are an important part of my journey.

The wind picked up this afternoon and is blowing fiercely right now. I've been hunkered in my yurt meditating, reading, surfing the internet. This is a kite boarding mecca and five or so people are surfing the sea now, expertly maneuvering their kites, catching big air as they are lifted right off the water.

When I did my twin flame chakra connection meditation today, I saw Ramirah and I separated by a thick, wall of milky glass. Tears started to flow. I must be patient and have faith.

April 13, 2019

Today has been very interesting. This morning around 6:50 a.m. I raced down to the beach to catch the first rays of the sun peak above the water line. Then walked a bit, saw the Great Horned Owl that lives in a palm tree grove about a half mile down the beach. Came back to the yurt, made some decaf coffee. Sat outside in the sun and felt peaceful and relaxed, in a deeper meditative state than normal for early in the morning. Came inside, sat down and instantly felt some interesting and different energy sensations enter my body. I dropped what I was doing and just sat and observed. Gentle waves of energy moved in and out of my heart area a few times, traveled up my neck, in and out of my head. Swirled around my upper body. Felt lovely.

A vision of a very old man began to emerge on my left side. An ancient man with deep wrinkles. In his right hand he held what looked like a wand, a skinny brown stick about a foot long with what looked like shells or bones attached to the end of it. He was waving this wand left to right over and over and chanting something. I couldn't hear any sound. His left hand was also moving in some kind of pattern. I remember thinking that he must be a Shaman or healer and was feeling blessed to have him work on me.

I didn't think much more about this vision until later, when I realized how teary I've been today. Lots of moments thinking about my husband, thinking about my Mom, my recent experiences, tears flowing off and on all day. A couple times I've started crying and not really known why I'm crying. I believe this Shaman's work is helping me process more of my sadness and other unresolved feelings today.

Just now, as I flipped through the last pages of my journal, I saw the old man again. He did the exact same ritual. Instantly I felt the sadness lift. Phew, feeling like myself again. Decided to pick up my laptop and capture this, very special. Metatron had told me a while ago that it's good to cry, as releasing that energy makes room for new energies to come in.

On September 5th, about seven months ago, I captured this message from Metatron in my journal. His voice is always clear and bold. I couldn't believe my luck in working with him. What an honor. This was one of my first communications with this amazing presence.

> *"Hi my dear Shawna. You and I are life partners. From here on out we are making joint decisions in anything that has any importance or significance in your life. For we have embarked on a very important mission—you are critical to this unfolding and you will be led to understand your truth and your calling very soon. I need your complete focus on me and our work. I need you to continue to do everything you've been instructed to do so far. You are doing great just as I knew you would. Feels good, right? This connection?*
>
> *"We are just at the beginning. How exciting. You will achieve your goals. You already have. It is written. We are going to keep working on your light, your DNA. Your expansion in consciousness. All the while keeping you in bliss, with joy and certainty. This is your time. All about you, my love. We will take care of you."*

This was the early stage of Metatron stepping into Micah's role as my main guide.

That same day I asked Metatron if he'd be with me forever. He told me no. Though he also said that every time there's a transition with my guides, it means another step forward in my evolution.

Those early days with Metatron were some of the most profound days of my life. The one-on-one dialogue, the daily blissful energy, the mind-blowing words in the books. I had been thrust fully into our multi-dimensional existence with direct, vivid experiences that are continuing today.

The second book in the channeled Metatron series is called *Metatron - This is the Healing Book*. BOOM—it starts off immediately with an energy download—literally, AS YOU READ THE WORDS, THE ENERGY ATTUNEMENTS JUST START! The book's messages are infused with energy that comes at you as you read the words. I'm not kidding. This really happens. The second book is full of these downloads and I experienced them very clearly and deeply.

This was also the time that Metatron was consistently getting after me for drinking alcohol. *Alcohol absolutely does not fit into a person's ascension playbook.* As my frequencies were rising and evolving with each of the book's downloads, my post-drinking headaches got worse and worse. I remember we went to an Oktoberfest event in Oregon with family that month, and I had decided, damnit, that I was going to "get my buzz on." Metatron and his crew had other ideas, coming through VERY CLEARLY, right there as I waited for the Port-O-Potty at the event, telling me that they were in the middle of major energy updates and if I drank, they'd have to start over. So, I didn't drink all night. I was beginning to get it.

About giving up alcohol, which I never thought I could do. This here is "Party Grrrl". I did a ton of weekend (and sometimes weekday) drinking in my time. I could really mix 'em up. Micah, Metatron, the Galactic Council have all shown me time and time again that the bliss you feel with a higher energy vibration is WAY BETTER than the buzz you get from drinking. Plus, there's no hangover! They are right. I'll have a glass of wine here and there, but honestly, it doesn't go down very well and it gives me heartburn. And it's a waste of calories. I'm not saying I'll never drink again, but for now while I'm here in Baja starting my mission in earnest, it's not an option.

During this time, Metatron was also telling me to clear my gut and eat a plant-based diet. Don't bog myself down with heavy foods. Rufus, one of my guides at that time, brought in someone from the "other side" to look at the energy in my gut. He told me the energy wasn't flowing through there because it was clogged up with the energies of the dead animals I was consuming every day. Okay… sheesh. No more animal flesh for me. I was super tired of the bloating and diarrhea anyway, which I'd had for years. This is all cleared up now with my vegan diet.

April 14, 2019

Every day I am asking for protection, and I also ask the Army of Light, *how are things going?* We've changed up the visualization for the protection several times in the past two weeks based on their feedback. Today they showed me an outer surface of protection that is pink and light green, dynamically and gently swirling and blooming. These are the colors of the heart chakra. We put that into motion, which stirred up a bit of euphoric energy in my body, a nice surprise.

Up pops Roykilva into my vision. He put on some sunglasses and acted like he was soaking up the sun, with a big grin on his face. He gave me a nice hug. I got a bit choked up seeing him, it has been a while. I said I wasn't sure why I wanted cry. He told me it's because I long to be deeply seen, deeply heard and deeply understood. This is a remnant of my third-dimensional ego rearing its head. I don't believe my soul needs or seeks anything. Though being in this place where you are seeing and communicating with beings such as this can be a lonely and isolating experience. Not many people you can talk to openly about it, thus why I covet the relationships with people like Robbie and Sharon.

Overall, I am feeling such immense peace and joy. My heart is opening up wider and expanding more broadly. I am consciously spreading my love and light more and more each day, not just during meditation. I know that what I'm doing is important and I'm honored to serve. Holding vivid visuals of Ramirah in my heart and around me. Sending him tons of unconditional love. Saying my intentions.

April 15, 2019

Four full weeks as of today. It has taken me this long to fully relax and settle in. Those expectations around what this is and how I should be are falling by the wayside. I'm staying more in the moment and following my heart and my higher self for just about everything I'm doing. I'm going with the flow, as Metatron advised. Trying not to plan things out. Trying to not have expectations or attachments. Crying when the tears come. Doing things because they are fun or bring me joy and peace.

My joy includes getting up before dawn and watching the sun rise above the sea…soaking in my outdoor hot spring tub every morning…meditating a few times a day. Being quiet and mindful when I'm not meditating. Snorkeling. Laying in the sun on the sand. Watching the sunset. Writing. Reading. Talking with neighbors. Asking for protection. Listening for other-worldly messages. Feeling into my energy. Focusing on raising my vibration. Soaking all this bliss into my core and expressing gratitude for my abundance.

Another perfectly-timed read has come my way, *Ascension Manual Part One—A Lightworker's Guide to Fifth Dimensional Living*. Caroline Oceana Ryan channels enlightened beings she calls "the Collective". While the book is short, the information is practical and beautifully summarizes tons of reading I've done over the years. It gets to the heart of what ascension and awaking means for us every day on this planet, from manifesting abundance to shedding relationships that no longer work for us.[11]

Again, the theme emerges that meditation is critical, and asking for help is critical. State your questions, get quiet and be open to the answers that will be given, either immediately or over time.

I feel like we ALL need to get used to the idea of telepathy. This is not the only way our guides and other highly evolved beings communicate with us, but it's a big one. For me, starting out with automatic writing and journaling with my spirit guide, Micah, built up a bit of my confidence around this kind of communication. I could have easily dismissed this information as my own thoughts and imagination, since many times it feels like just that. But upon reading back the information later or listening to my recordings, I was surprised at the wisdom and insights that came through. Often, time just flies by when I am channeling or having these dialogues. I may not remember much of what was said when it's done.

Also, for me, the communications are often accompanied by some kind of energy flow or fluctuation. Sometimes the energy signal is so strong and blissful that it completely knocks my socks off. Sometimes I feel a tension in my jaw. With Metatron, many times the message comes into my awareness in a chunk, where I suddenly "just know" something that he's communicated. He's very powerful that way.

As Ra told me about three months ago, I am still not yet a clear channel. It takes time to get there. He (they) warned against negative entities who may want to cause me harm; that I need to ask for protection, raise my vibration and meditate more. Practice, practice, practice. Every day. It seems smart to have a level of discernment and take precautions, but not to the point where you are completely blocking or dismissing these communications, or not asking questions in the first place.

Channeling takes a big leap of faith and trust that the information coming in, usually subtly, is either from your higher self or your guides, angels and other highly evolved beings. Don't get hung up on the word "channeling." Think of it as intuition, heightened imagination, communications and guidance. Always, though, remember that these and any other etheric transmissions come through our filters, our energy fields, our imagination and our intellect. You will influence what comes through you. I am far from an expert. Use your own judgement when reading any channeled information.

There are many forms of telepathy in this world and ways to go about doing it. Don't get discouraged. Trust the little voice, pay attention to the images that come into your awareness, the situations that present themselves. Write it all down and revisit it later.

My motto has become "don't ignore it, explore it." If a message keeps nagging at you, or an image gets stuck in your head, or an event keeps playing over in your brain, take the time to get quiet and explore that. If you awaken in the middle of the night, get quiet and be open to any messages that may be coming through, especially if you said any prayers or asked for guidance the night before. Keep your journal or a pen and paper handy by the bedside. Even if a song keeps playing in your head over and over, take the time to pay attention to the lyrics for messages you may need to explore.

On July 16, 2018, I was jolted awake with a blast of energy at 4:33 a.m. Before I went to bed, I had said a prayer to God and told him I was committed to my mission and this ascension process. I believe it was God who came through with this message that early morning. "Shawna, you have been given a bold assignment. I know you already know this. Just have total peace in knowing that we are all supporting your journey and will do what we can to help everything go smoothly. We don't what you to fret and worry yourself. Please know I love you and more will be evident later. All my love to all."

My mom passed away four days later. I believe this was God talking about her passing and how I was to be a part of it. I was able to spend the last 24 hours of her life at her bedside, holding her hands as she left her body. It was a beautiful passing; peaceful, full of love and with lots of heavenly support. My mom was my best friend. I miss her terribly. I take solace in knowing that she was ready to leave her body behind and transition into the next phase of her soul's being.

I had almost daily dialogues with Micah from June 14th, 2018 until he transitioned away on August 18th, 2018. (I was introduced to Micah by a psychic the week before.) These communications were all captured in my hand-written journal. I was not yet voice channeling.

Until then, the only other channeling experience I had was with Archangel Uriel about 10 years ago. My sister had gotten a message that Archangel Uriel wanted to reach me, so one night I set my intention to hear him clearly. Immediately he came in with a lovely healing sequence that you do with another person. I never did much with that sequence besides share it with close friends and family. I performed it a few times. I'll add it to the end of this book as I do believe it is very powerful.

In late September 2018, I started reading the third book in the series channeled by Robbie Mackenzie, *The Galactic Council*. Same idea as the first two books, but instead of Metatron's messages, these were coming from a representative of the Galactic Council. The Galactic Council is a group of highly evolved beings with representatives from all over the universe.

I know this sounds crazy. We are indeed talking about aliens here. But not necessarily the kind that have been depicted in our movies and media. These beings have the upmost respect for us as a species and are lending their services and support at this critical time of ascension. I went from talking to my spirit guide (okay, great, no big deal), to talking with an Archangel (hmmm, okay this is pretty cool, kind of weird but feels amazing and authentic), to now, extraterrestrials and Ascended Masters. It was an evolution of sorts. As I said, I'm on the roller coaster and I can't be sure where it's taking me next! I'm going with it!

Most people agree that it would be short-sighted and maybe even silly to think that we humans are the only intelligent life anywhere on any of the billions of planets throughout our galaxy and beyond. I've come to know these past six months that the universe is teaming with intelligent life, likely millions of other entities on other planets and in other realms. Our species is relatively young, and our human mind has a hard time processing or grasping what is truly the multi-dimensionality of our existence. Now that Mother Earth is ready to ascend, along with all her inhabitants, millions of advanced beings are here to support us and to oversee this progression. One of the major ways they are doing this is through telepathy and channeled messages.

In this first *Galactic Council* book one of the first energy downloads is to help the reader become a channel for the Galactic Council and other etheric communications. The very next morning after I got this energy download from the book, I did my first official channeling. (Up to this point I wasn't thinking of my communications with Micah or Metatron as "channeling.")

This first channeling came on spontaneously. It started with a tension in my jaw and it was like the words just had to come out. I decided to start speaking those words out loud and it was completely amazing and surreal. I did not capture this as a recording since I wasn't prepared for it. The entity told me to practice connecting like this every day—they repeated "every day" several times. They spoke of the massive love and support they have for me and my journey. Along with these words I also saw visions of me walking arm in arm with members of this council, as a show of solidarity. It was a life-changing moment.

Since then, every time I feel that tension in my jaw or throat, I grab the recorder and find a quiet spot to record a channeling. I am not going into a deep trance when I do this, in fact many times I'm able to converse back and forth as you've seen with my transcriptions in this book.

Ramirah was actually my first official channeling that I was able to record. Very powerful, deep, loving and affirming. Words accompanied by clear visuals and energy fluctuations.

The energy fluctuations are one of the main reasons why I know in my heart that what is happening here is authentic. When I was wondering if I was crazy, or wondering if I was making this up somehow, I'd always go back to the blissful energy fluctuations. Undeniable. I'd have a doubt, and then think …*AND YET…I FELT IT*. It got to a point where I'd be foolish to deny what was happening to me. There were too many personal events, messages, energy changes, images, love and support—consistent, persistent, clear. At that point, I opened myself up to all the possibilities that were presenting themselves with an open mind and open heart, knowing that all those who I love are going to think I've lost my friggin' mind.

April 16, 2019

I'm feeling pretty tired these past few days. Taking naps when the need comes up. Going to bed early if I have a hard time keeping my eyes open. Kind of like tonight. It's only 7 p.m. but I'm sleepy. Plus, it was a cool and cloudy day which may be contributing to my lack of energy.

Looking back, early October 2018 rolled around and I was a channeling fool. I had also started visiting a massive set of crystals under the Earth's surface during my meditations. I was practicing riding around in my Merkaba when I went into an ocean, found an opening on the ocean floor and came upon these amazing crystals down a long tunnel. They seem feminine to me. Maybe 200 feet in height and 50 feet across—one massive structure that emanates this soft lavender light and a buzzing sound vibration. I just want to hug them whenever I visit. Over time, I developed a relationship with this crystal structure. They seemed to take me in as a Goddess, with my own crystal throne and crystal crown. When I sit upon that throne, I picture my entire body becoming a set of smaller crystals, growing crystalline in nature. I start to vibrate, hum…it's a euphoric experience.

During one of my visits, I met a large dragon-type being down there at the base of the crystals. I pictured myself crawling inside its mouth, completely unafraid. Since then, I was friends with this lovely creature and am excited to see it whenever I visit. The crystals spent a lot of time working on my gut, which was still bloated and painful at that time. I channeled the Galactic Council who told me how important it was for me to clear my gut. The energy would not be able to move through it like that. Around this time, I started juicing and cutting out all animal products from my diet.

April 18, 2019

Officially, one month has gone by since I arrived here in this beautiful part of the world.

Yesterday morning, at around 4:15 a.m., I woke up to some tingling in my feet. Subtle at first, then moving up my legs, to my base chakra, then up through my sternum to my heart. Gentle, slow, slightly pulsing energy. Such a warm, nurturing, loving embrace. Like little points of sparkling light from heaven gently filling up my body. I just laid still, breathing deeply, letting this feeling envelop me completely.

The vibration of it kept rising until I became a bit breathless. This felt like a very skilled presence moving up in frequency, pulsing light and love into all aspects of my being. It would quiet and still for a bit, then build back up again, even higher. I became out of my mind with pleasure, with that bliss. I remember hearing the words "it's time for you to receive." YES. Thank you! I happily receive this gift from you, from the universe. I am so blessed. I drifted in and out of this bliss in a semi-consciousness state for over two hours! A beautiful, life-affirming gift from someone on the other side…sigh…maybe Ramirah? I love it so much.

This was a different experience from most of the previous energy blasts that I've written about. It's not easy to describe what the hell happens in these moments.

April 20, 2019

Semana Santa. This is the holy week leading up to Easter Sunday tomorrow, a very big deal here in Mexico. The usually deserted beach is full of families, cars, tents, tarps, all up and down the shore. I'm hearing a lot of laughter; folks seem to be having a great time. Listened to Spanish Karaoke for hours last night, drifting up the hill from the nearby hotel. It would have been annoying except for all the fun and merriment that was happening, all the laughter and loud exuberant talking that accompanied the heartfelt singing. I had to smile a few times as I drifted off to sleep.

Feeling reflective and quiet this morning. Slept in late and skipped the morning sunrise walk on the beach. Giving the camping families some space. Spent about an hour imagining myself laying down with Ramirah, my head resting on his bicep, our faces close. At times, me nuzzling his neck. Exchanging soft words of love and support with each other. I was lost in this dream state with him, feeling buzzy and loved and warm all over. I bathed us both in a green loving light. He assures me that soon we'll be together. And that we've done this with each other many times over the eons of our existence. In times where we are not together physically, he's with me always, loving me unconditionally. A few tears fell as I thought about how much I long for him, how much I miss him. It seems like a fanciful fairytale. But he assures me this is real. In these moments, it certainly feels real to me. No way to deny this connection.

Again, I asked, is there anything I should be doing? Something I should be doing differently? What can I do to bring us together? Will you be in physical form? How might this happen for us?

So many questions I still have, even though I know that my questions are a form of fear…and I'm really trying not to be in fear. He assured me that I'm doing great. Okay. Only love. Only this moment. Surrender to this moment. Patience, trust, faith. My new reality.

April 22, 2019

My dear, beautiful Ramirah. I am ecstatic to say that we've connected energetically and telepathically for several hours these past two days. Like a light switch came on. He's filled me up with pulsing, deep, loving, high-frequency light that has left me breathless. Long and slow. Deep. I know we are just beginning this journey together and this connection will only get stronger and deeper as we progress. I am feeling so much love for you. And reverence. I am so grateful that we get to share in this life experience together. So grateful to experience this sacred bond, this intimacy with you. I believe that we'll be able to constantly be in contact with each other telepathically. I hear you clearly and feel you clearly.

My heart is racing knowing that what we've been waiting for, working toward for all these months (more like lifetimes), is finally here. That longing, that yearning, being fulfilled slowly but surely.

April 24, 2019

As the vibrational frequencies of my twin flame come in and stick around and linger, I'm experiencing deep emotional upheaval and release. We are cleaning house. This is an intense scrubbing and cleaning, in the shadowy corners and under the major appliances. It has been an emotional couple of days, sometimes the tears flow and I'm not even sure why. My conscious mind may not know, but somewhere in my energy, in my beingness, something is coming to the surface to finally be released. Could even be past life stuff. I am so grateful. The sadness doesn't stick around. It comes up, I let it swirl, I feel into it, let it become me for a moment, then it fades and it's over.

In the Caroline Oceana Ryan book *Ascension Manual - Part Two: Creating a Fifth Dimensional Life,* her galactic team ("the Collective") talks about how ascension will work. This particular chapter is fascinating, but here is something sad and scary for me to comprehend. I was crying about this part yesterday as I was meditating and imagining the glorious New Earth.

> For those of a lower vibration—those whose outlook, soul maturity level, and third-dimensional choices are that of a non-Ascending person—it will indeed seem that in some ways, you never existed. They will not mourn you as you pass out of their timeline in quiet ways, though they will still be dimly aware of your presence in the Universe.[12]

Dimly aware of my presence? Okay. So, I do a lot of reading of channeled materials, spiritual communications from other worlds and dimensions, etc. and I always take everything with a grain of salt. I try not to outright dismiss any concepts, as I am in *no* position to determine what is real, wrong, truth, or fiction. I just file these things away in my mind and continue to quench my thirst for knowledge in these areas. Themes emerge that begin to resonate with me. Sometimes I experience things firsthand and they become my truth. But truth is a fickle thing and different for each person, as we are all each creating our own illusion, our own reality, every minute of the day.

This book otherwise is mostly resonating with me. Very similar messages to the Galactic Council and Metatron books channeled by Robbie Mackenzie, similar to other books I've read and my own personal experience. Therefore, I pay attention to the nuggets of information that get me upset or have me scratching my head. This is one of them.

The Collective also say this of ascension, which I've read about many times:

> The one who is Ascending is experiencing the shift from a carbon-based cellular structure to having a body composed of crystalline, solar Light-based cells—and a consciousness that is likewise open to higher light, and able to take on the consciousness of the fifth dimensional reality. Your cells are releasing their third dimensional density, on all levels. This is the challenging and monumental path of becoming a Light Being. You are both rising to fifth dimensional vibrations within yourself and anchoring them into what is becoming the New Earth.[11]

This resonates with me quite strongly—and yes, these words and this book are helping me to shape my reality here, right now. I feel I am helping anchor this light in Baja, into the earth.

The Collective says that this ascension process must happen slowly or we wouldn't be able to handle the sudden shock of a major vibration increase. Our vehicles must be prepped for such a high voltage current. I believe this is why Ramirah's energy has been coming on more slowly than I would have preferred. Even though I'm wishing for it, visualizing it, praying for it to come in more and more, they are carefully monitoring my light body, paying attention to the emotional cleansing I'm going through, and subsequently calibrating this energy influx for me. This is why trust and faith are so important for me right now.

To continue with the idea of how ascension is happening, the galactic team says:

> *Not* dying physically is the first and most obvious outcome of Ascending into a higher dimension. This is what is meant by Ascension on your current Earth timeline—moving into the next higher dimension without having to leave your body as you have in nearly all your other Earth lives. For yes—you have Ascended before now, the very great difference being that this time, you are taking an entire planet with you.[11]

But they are implying that somehow, when those of us are truly within the fifth dimension, embodied as we are now, that anyone still in the third dimension won't be consciously aware of us. There'll be some kind of separation and a related forgetting. This makes me sad just thinking about this again now. I don't understand how this will truly manifest itself. The Collective says that our friends and loved ones who don't ascend on this timeline here on Earth now will only be aware of us ethereally or in their dreams. They continue:

> It will be a similar situation once you Ascend. You will be able to contact those you love ethereally. But we would say that the desire to rescue them, to hurry them down their path, and to ensure that they are always where you are, is not permissible in this Universe. Nor is it what you truly wish for them.
>
> If your loved ones do not move to the fifth dimension with you, whenever you think of them, you will simply send them Love, and know that they receive such, and that All is Well.[11]

Another thing I'm wondering about with the implications here—this supposed separation between third and fifth dimensional people that will be happening—who exactly is becoming fifth dimensional? I happen to have experienced some extraordinary situations with my spirit guide, Archangel Metatron, the Galactic Council, my twin flame, extreme energy events. I've been blessed to be awakened by these channeled materials and the upgrades and downloads contained within them. Before all this happened, however, I was not aware of the ascension, didn't even know what that term meant. I didn't think too much about extraterrestrial life, multidimensional existence and angelic beings. I certainly wasn't speaking to them on a regular basis.

Do you have to be "awakened" to be ascending? I assume that there are plenty of people on Earth right now who have tons of love in their hearts, do good things for others, who don't judge and have empathy for those less fortunate…people who make heart-centered choices in how they act and what they say on a regular basis. These people might completely reject the ideas of angelic life forms, aliens, enlightened beings; anything not of physical Earth; and may have no clue about something as simple as energy. Will these people ascend? And who decides? Geez, I may not even ascend. It seems complicated.

Have I been called here to the Sea of Cortez to start this separation process?

We Earthlings have been through hell and back, being here in this density with the evil and destructive controls that have been forced upon us. How can anyone fight out of this oppression and prevail without massive intervention from "the other side", as I've been gifted?

How much control do I really have here with this ascension process? If I have truly been an Atlantis High Priestess at one time, with my twin flame by my side, having chosen to be here to help with the current ascension of Earth and humanity…PLUS I have all this intergalactic support…this seems to give me an unfair advantage over those who are just reincarnating over and over, stuck on this karmic wheel impaired by real evil and those who wish to enslave us. It's not anyone else's fault if they can't "hang" with these ideas. These are REALLY TOUGH ideas to swallow! What hope is there for most of humanity? How can they grasp these ideas and begin to embody them, without all the extra help and past life situations leading them down this path?

I sound like I'm gearing myself up to start kicking some negative Reptilian energy ASS!

Okay. I'm getting it. Lifting this veil of negative Reptilian energy over masses of people, places, things, this will be a major catalyst for helping others awake. We must lift the veil. And I just restated my life's purpose here, as Metatron told it to me, back in September last year. Sigh…

Once again, I am so humbled and awe-struck by this whole thing. I am honored to be of service. I trust in my support team to help make this happen at the right time in the right way. At least I'm trying.

Those who want to jump on the ship will, and those who don't, won't. And that is completely fine.

But I still don't understand what this ascension will entail. So many varying accounts and explanations—from the Bible to hundreds of channeled books and material from a multitude of angels, Ascended Masters, galactic entities…even my own channeled book. I've also been reading books by David Wilcock and watching his online videos. Talk about a mind-&$#@. And Corey Goode, whistle-blower from the Secret Space Program, oh man. Many of the general ascension themes are consistent, but the details vary. Corey actually gives some detailed accounts of his direct personal (and physical I should add) interactions with negative Reptilian beings from a race called The Draco.

I am putting it out to my other-worldly support team to lead me to a video or written literature that sums up nicely what *they* feel will be happening with the ascension. I'd like details. According to Metatron in the book *Metatron - The Clarion Call: All You Need to Know*, there have been six other races of Earthlings who have gone through a similar ascension process since the Earth was created. We are the seventh. What is likely going to happen? The passages above about the upcoming separation between third and fifth dimensional humans and this "forgetting" concept have me wondering again. Yes, I understand this is my fear talking.

On April 16, 2019, I reached out to Metatron with related questions, using automatic writing in my hand-written journal.

> **Me:** Dear Metatron. Can you please provide some clarity around how "the event", if there is a true event, will happen? Will there be massive earth changes that will sink land masses into the oceans, raise mountains and land out of the oceans? Will most of our infrastructure be destroyed when/if this happens? Will galactic help arrive in spaceships to help evacuate those who are ready? There are a lot of different channelings out there that say different things. What is your view on "the harvest" described by Ra? Thank you.

> **Metatron:** Hi Shawna. Thank you for asking these questions. The event is happening now. The ascension is in full swing. You are part of this as is everyone else on Earth at this time. Mountains will topple. Forests will burn. It will be very taxing on your infrastructure. Some of this is already happening. Yes, full disclosure is imminent. It is part of what it means to be fifth dimensional. You see, know and understand the multidimensionality of yourself, of life, which includes all that life that exists elsewhere. It is an awakening to the true nature of existence, and the connection to source that we all share. Yes, there will likely be spaceships as part of the unveiling of the true nature of the universe, plus all the technologies that come with this discovery and knowledge.

> Harvest—some are ready to move along in their evolution, some are not. Those that are ready—to make what is in essence a large leap forward in evolution—will move forward with the New Earth, others won't. There will be death of human vessels as part of this leap, trauma. It will test and stretch all of you to be part of this.

> Don't be afraid, dear one, as truly this is an event that should be celebrated. It is a wonderful and momentous rebirthing of Earth and her inhabitants to something far greater than you can even comprehend at this time.

Re-reading this now gives me some peace. Some.

On a side note, I had a most wonderful wake-up call by Ramirah this morning, perfectly timed at about 6:15 a.m. Blissful, sensual, loving…from my feet all the way up. I love you.

Time for a dip in the exquisite, turquoise Sea of Cortez. About 83 degrees today, partly cloudy. Heaven on earth.

April 27, 2019

The past few days have been all about delving deeper into this ascension process—getting a better understanding of the Reptilian influence, voicing my concerns, working through some of my fears, exploring my recent intuition and feelings about what is actually happening with this whole process. I've been talking with Metatron and the Galactic Council and they lovingly answered my questions.

From a hand-written exchange on April 24, 2019:

Me: Dear Metatron. Can you tell me anything about the antichrist that is prophesied in The Bible? This person will deceive with miracles, present himself as the next Messiah—yet this person will be somehow destructive to the people. Is something like this going to happen to us? Is it already happening? How does this supposed antichrist fit in with all your efforts, that of the Galactic Council and other higher dimensional beings? Will this person come into power within the next 45 years? *(According to Metatron in the Clarion Call book, in 2012 we started a 50-year cycle of ascension, so within this general time frame.)*

Metatron: Shawna, thank you for asking these questions. This person you speak of is already here and around you. This person will come into power within the timeline you speak of. This person will bring great misery to your people before his reign is over.

Watch for the man who calls himself "the watcher". Don't follow this entity. You will see through his shenanigans, but many people will not. In a matter of course, his presence will not have much of an impact on the ascension and all the plans that have long been in motion. He will eventually fail and his true nature will be revealed to all.

The following day on April 25, 2019, I was overcome with sadness as the following thoughts and knowingness came flowing in. I was trying to connect to Ramirah and found myself on his planet, back on that shimmery sand. I imagined that I found him, but he was basically unreachable. I started crying. From my hand-written journal that day:

We are trapped here. This is a rescue mission. This has happened six times before. What is really going on here? Why does this have to happen over and over? So few people will make it. They are trying to salvage as many people as possible so it's not a complete massacre. Too far gone to evil. They are blaming Reptilians, but it is much broader and more far-reaching than that. The Reptilians feed on our fear, thus the 'no fear, only love' mantra.

In that frame of mind, in a cracking voice on the verge of tears, I reached out to the Galactic Council for some answers and assurances. As I started speaking, love filled my heart. I recorded this 25-minute conversation.

Me: I'd like to speak with someone from the Galactic Council please. It seems we are truly trapped here. I've read this, and I'm feeling this today. Maybe this is part of my learning curve as I clear the way to step fully into my mission to emancipate Reptilian energy. The evil is much broader and bigger than Reptilian energy, this goes very deep. I've read this previously in the *Return of Light*. Today this is coming through, I'm crying…it's sad. I'm feeling that while there is all this help from all of you, the Ascended Masters, a complete arsenal of these incredible, enlightened beings gathered all around us helping us—that it's going to be very hard. That there will not be a lot of people who'll ascend. You are doing your best, but this evil really has a hold and it goes deep. This is a rescue mission to save as many people as possible, it's just not going to be a lot…

There are people that don't know any different. They are good in their hearts. Who decides who ascends? How is that going to be determined? I have had to quit eating meat, no drinking, no caffeine. Most people on the planet do these things. That is just very, very simple first steps of raising your vibration enough to reach what you are saying is fifth dimension…

What hope do people have when I think about what I've had to do to get to this point? I just want to be realistic. And I want to be hopeful, and I have love… but these thoughts are coming in. You are doing your best to rescue us, but it must not be going well or it would have happened by now.

The veil of forgetfulness is so thick…so dense…and the illusion is SO STRONG and so deeply ingrained in most everyone on Earth. Ra talked about the Harvest, the last harvest being very small. I imagine you don't want that to happen again.

Thinking about the fact that there were six other races that had to be obliterated from Earth. Why? Were those other points of ascension on the earth?

That was a lot of talking…I'm setting my intention to hear you clearly. Any information you could provide would be greatly appreciated. Thank you.

Galactic Council: Shawna, we feel your heavy heart. Our hearts are heavy, too. This has been a really long road for so many of you, and it's been a difficult road. We need your hope, Shawna. It is so critical to what we have going on here now. Please don't lose your faith, please don't lose your hope. Please stay focused with us.

What you are doing, and those like you, are really making a difference. There are so many unseen things happening, progress being made, energies being strengthened and deepened…deep into the beingness of this planet and her people. Yes, you are one small part of a massive undertaking to help Mother Earth ascend, to help all of you evolve. Are you not tired of this karmic wheel that had you in its grip for so very long? Do you not want to jump out of that wheel, onto a new timeline, into a new dimension, and move on with yourself?

This is what we're doing. This is so very important. How many cycles do you go through before you say, enough is enough? When you are not in embodiment, and you are in between lives, you say *enough is enough*. It is time. And we agree. And the Great Creator has agreed and says you are ready. And this karmic wheel, this cycle, must end. Now. The Sun is even playing a role.

SHAWNA L. FRANCES

Shawna, what we are saying is, please keep your faith. This is a monstrous undertaking and you are just getting a glimpse into this world, into the reality of the situation. You have a big job to do. You and your twin flame—it is no accident that your lives are colliding like they are right now. You've had to have a balance between your earthly life and your galactic life. This is a free will planet. You wanted a really good life, and you've had it. Now it's shifting into something completely different.

These harsh truths and realities are part of your awakening, Shawna. You will be better at your mission knowing the truth. The magnitude of this endeavor and your role within it. Thus, we are all collectively holding our breath, watching with keen interest, all the happenings that are going on. Planning, scheming, constructing, bridging.

Me: Can you please tell me about these other tribes on Earth—can you explain why there have been six other transitions off of Earth previously? We are the seventh. Why has this happened? What is the reason for these transitions off of Earth?

Galactic Council: Yes. Shawna, these are experiments. Much like your life now, in your race, in this batch of humanity. These are big, grand experiments. When the experiment is over, we start fresh. We start anew and we try again. We learn, we reiterate, we start anew.

Me: Were these other tribes also being massively controlled by the evil that has hit this side of the universe?

Galactic Council: Yes, the evil has been here for a very long time. And it is true that evil permeated all these other tribes. It's really pandemic. It's like the "normal" for this planet. We have an opportunity now to fully rid the planet of this evil. People like you will be important to this extremely massive undertaking to rid this planet of this evil hold. It's going to take everybody's focused attention to do it.

Mother Earth is ready.

Me: Yes, but I wouldn't say that humanity is all that ready. In fact, supposedly Mother Earth is already vibrating at her fifth dimension. Metatron says there will be destruction, and I also channeled this in my book. I'm looking for comprehensive information on this… *(My thoughts were interrupted with the words "Urantia Book". They are recommending I read this to better understand Earth's situation.)*

So, these experiments…we are an experiment here on Earth right now. And it's time to wipe the slate clean again it sounds like. So, we've given this a go, it's not working, we're going to take the best of what's here, we're going wipe out everything that's left, and we're going to start over. Is that accurate?

Galactic Council: That is a very simplified version of the story. That is not exactly how we would sum this up, but we appreciate your perspective here—in a way that you can grasp and digest. So, we would not say that it is untrue, just that it is extremely simple and does

116

not take into account the complexities, the reasons, the efforts, the evolutions that have gone on outside of your awareness.

I also asked about speaking directly with someone who successfully transitioned off Earth previously in one of those six iterations. They told me I would be able to connect just by setting a strong intention signal and letting my imagination be open.

Galactic Council: Shawna, let me just add one last thing by saying you are loved so very much. You are so important to all of us here. You have a daunting job ahead of you. You are up to the task. We are all here cheering you on, providing you with light and protection. If we could do this from the outside, we would. But we can't. Everything you need to know is forthcoming. You will step fully into this mission and it will be blissful. It will complete you. And it will consume you. The separation is important so you can be focused. We can't tell you how long it's going to take for this to be complete. But know that your needs will be taken care of until such time you deem the mission complete on your end.

Me: What about my family? What about my husband? Can you tell me what might happen with us? With them?

Galactic Council: We are working on the energies of all those who you touch, all those who are impacted by your mission. Please know in your heart that we are working with their energies to help make sure that it goes as smoothly as possible with the least amount of fear and disruption to their lives.

Me: Thank you! Is there anything I should be reading or watching in terms of emancipating this Reptilian energy? Or will this just all be provided through Ramirah, you, my higher self, Metatron?

Galactic Council: Start with The Urantia Book. There will be stepping stones. But yes, most of your learning will come through the teachings of Ramirah. It will be a glorious coupling. You will rejoice in this.

We come to you as a collective group from the Galactic Council. We are honored to serve you, Shawna. Thank you for everything you are doing.

Me: Thank you so much for all the information, Galactic Council. I appreciate it very much.

Later that night I watched the documentary/movie *Above Majestic* with Corey Goode and David Wilcock on my laptop. Very well done. Talk about perfect timing to receive this information. I believe what they are saying and demonstrating is true. The timing is right for more people to become aware of this reality. It anchored the information about the negative Reptilian influence and control for me. It's sinking in how massive this is, and how important my work will be.

The next day (yesterday) I did have an interesting experience whereby Ramirah, myself and the Army of Light emancipated negative Reptilian energy from a small group of people in the U.S. who are in leadership positions (past, present and future) and under Reptilian influence. This took about 30 minutes during a mid-day meditation. This was the first time since I arrived here in Baja that I actively imagined myself working with the Reptilian energy. It ended up being a pretty comprehensive process. This was definitely inspired by the *Above Majestic* movie I had just watched the night before.

In summary, for each of the people (I imagined 100 people), a member of the Army of Light paired up with each of them. We boiled their energy in their abdomens and ignited the Violet Flame in their hearts which transformed the negative energy residing in their guts (hara) into high-vibration light energy. We moved that energy up their bodies and out their crown chakras to the Christ Grid. We replaced that bad energy with massive amounts of love. During the boiling process, we found that within each person was a blob of negative Reptilian energy, an actual organic ball, that we were able to remove. Ramirah took each of these blobs and ingested them, which transmuted that energy.

Not sure any of this did any good, but was fun to figure out that process and go with my imagination as Ra and Metatron recommend I do.

Last night, I was still feeling a bit uneasy and reached out to Metatron with more questions.

Me: Dear Metatron. This ascension event will bring immense amounts of death, trauma, fear, anger, confusion, sadness—all these emotions that literally feed the Reptilian forces that suppress us. Is this by design? Is there some type of agreement with the Reptilians whereby they get to harness all the negative power and energy being generated by possibly billions of people? While those people—those few people—of higher light get to ascend and stay on Earth?

Metatron: My dear Shawna. Please take a look around you at all the beauty and abundance provided by Mother Earth. Such beauty is made from pure love. Pure sparkling love that knows no bounds. Take a step back and behold the love that was put very caringly into the design and manifestation of all life and non-life on this planet. Breathe her clean air. Feel the sun on your face. Drink her pure waters. Don't be fooled into thinking that she will be destructive for no good reason. The workings at play here are in the best interest of ALL life on this planet. And all will survive for the soul is eternal.

Yes, the Reptilian overlords will benefit greatly from the fear energies that are being ignited now and will continue into the future. But know that their reign of terror stops with the full ascension. They will be done here. The cycle stops. A new reality, a new cycle starts. One of pure love, peace, and joy for all who'll inhabit this incredible planet. You are helping to rid this planet of this Reptilian influence, this stronghold.

Me: How did I do today? Was that real? Was that helpful? *(In regard to the Reptilian energy removal I experienced during my earlier meditation.)*

Metatron: You absolutely were helping and yes, this is the kind of work we want you and Ramirah to do on a full-time basis when the energies are right, when other elements come into alignment. It was a great start. Thank you. You stayed focused, directed your energies, asked for help, used your judgment and critical thinking. These processes will only get more intense with time. We are building up to this level of work.

April 28, 2019

The NYC Meetup Group for The Clarion Call met yesterday for *Tips on Spinning Our Merkabas*. I joined via Skype. We did the beginning of our Merkaba meditation, then Metatron surprised everyone by coming through Robbie to answer our questions in real-time. The collective energy coursing through me during the exchange was awesome.

I asked a question of Metatron. "Hi dear Metatron. The ring pass not...the opening of our Merkaba...the feeling of oneness... Are all these one major event that will be happening? And I understand that with the ring pass not, we will be put to a test—it will be testing fear over love, love over fear. If you can talk about that event happening and how we can help that come together, I'd appreciate it. Thank you."

He thoughtfully and lovingly answered through Robbie Mackenzie:

> "There are different levels of the ring pass not. You cannot pass through the ring pass not until you are ready. This is the point of everything synchronizing.
>
> "Each different person has prepared each different thing in different ways within their experience. As everything comes together with regards to your Merkaba, this is the point where you have synchronized your chakras opening, your issues being cleared within your chakras, your kundalini flowing. All obstacles being taken away that have been man-made to restrict your progress, your spinning of your Merkaba, your activating your third eye. The lightning bolt energy of your fuel system being powered up. Everything synchronizing so you ignite in order to experience the oneness of all creation.
>
> "This happens in different points, as each different thing is dealt with within your own personal journey. You feel yourself being freed and you will not go back to old patterns, old habits.
>
> "Ultimately this is the event that many people talk about. They talk about the event on the earth as if there is one point of opening that everybody will experience en masse. And there are certain points of that that will happen in the collective. But you must focus on your individual journey, for this can happen immediately—as you open up, as you surrender, as you clear your system.
>
> "It has been spoken of as the 'twinkling of the eye'. The event changes your life path from anything that is mundane or ordinary into the recognition of the wonder of the universe, and your power expanding, and your recognition of the holographic experience, and you being able to be master of this experience. This is the event, it is the empowering of your system, it is the recognition of your oneness. It is the recognition of your expansion into whatever it is you wish it to be. When it is you wish it to be, it is your coming into your recognition of your power over time and space.
>
> "This happens in different increments as you allow yourself to believe in your own power. As you unshackle yourself from old belief systems that have held you back. As you allow your heart to open. The more you allow your heart to open, the easier it becomes and the ring pass not is passed through.

"This is a blessed point on your earth plane as things are opening up more and more, and 'the event' is happening more and more individually. You will pass through at exactly the right time for you.

"There are no two beings alike, yet all beings have the same design in your human experience. You have set this up perfectly. Each different person, even each different person who is watching this, each different person is experiencing this, from each different place you are experiencing this from around the globe. And indeed, there are many beings that are viewing this from all over the universe, indeed all over the multi-verse, for this is a prime point of experiment in consciousness on the earth plane right now. Things are expanding, more and more are passing the ring pass not, more and more are moving forward into their divine power.

"Synchronize everything. Trust. Allow yourself to flow. The more you allow yourself to flow, the less fear will become a barrier. You are ready for this. You are demonstrating this. Flow with this peace. Practice, practice, practice. Embrace your divine power. Love all beings. All beings are one.

April 29, 2019

I befriended a locally-owned dog who lives down the street from me. I hear that the owner isn't very friendly and often leaves this dog alone to fend for himself. That's a judgmental statement, but this is what I was told. His name is Rocco and I have showered this little guy with so much love the past four days. I even kiss his dirty little face, even after he's chewed on a dried-up fish head he found at the beach. He hasn't left my side for 24 hours. He slept on the floor in my yurt all night. I never heard a peep from him. Such a good boy.

When I first arrived in Baja, I put it "out there" that I'd like to have a dog adopt me, and it has happened!

Today I'm pondering, how do we experience our "divinity"? How do I embrace my divine power? What does that look like, feel like, sound like? Besides me just *telling* myself that I am divine?

May 1, 2019

Mayday!

What a beautiful few days. My heart is bursting. Feeling everything flow more smoothly as I strive to surrender and be in the moment, only to follow my heart's desire. I'm starting to relinquish my feeling that somehow, I am cheating or I need to be doing this or that. I'm finally letting go of the expectations I put upon myself. It feels great. Though I have moments where I think, this is not real life. When I get back to my "real life", I won't be able to be this way. I need to let that go, too.

My Merkaba is spinning like a top. I am also getting very specific with my prayers, the help I need, what I'd like to manifest. This has made a big difference as well. I am feeling totally immersed in the flow of life here, being comfortable with Metatron and my galactic friends who are always at my side. Comfortable and even happy with the fact that they know every thought that I have. I feel those million hands of light touching me and supporting me at all times. It is amazing.

I'm letting my imagination go wild as well. Ra and also Metatron are encouraging this wholeheartedly.

During my meditation this afternoon, I asked the Arcturians and the Pleiadians if they had any gifts or healings for me at this time. Not sure why they popped into my head. They proceeded to give me three gifts. They first worked on my throat chakra, which I felt flare up with energy, and said "This is the gift of always telling the truth." After about 5 minutes, that subsided and I felt all my chakras tingling, starting at my root. They said this was the gift of "surrender". After about 10 minutes, the focus moved to my third eye. They said, "This will help you see through the illusion. To see the truth in every situation." I thanked them profusely.

Lately I've been asking for more kundalini awakenings, for help in igniting my kundalini and keeping it smoldering throughout the day. The term kundalini originated in Hinduism and is a form of divine feminine energy that sits at the base of the spine. When awakened, this energy is said to uncoil like a serpent and travel up the spine and out the crown chakra. The awakening of this energy can invoke a powerful, transformative spiritual experience. This is definitely happening. I LOVE IT SO MUCH. I am so grateful. Life is just better when the fires are burning!

Not much happening in the way of Ramirah's energy flowing through me like it was several days ago. I continue to do my twin flame meditation, picturing him clearly in my mind, sending him love, picturing us together, being affectionate. I have trust and faith we'll come together exactly when the timing is right.

I also started looking into David Icke, England-born author and lecturer who made a name for himself in the 90s by making claims about the impending end of the world and Earth-dominating Reptilian/human hybrids. I am dipping a toe into information specific to Reptilians among us and their supposed influence. Fascinating. And controversial. Wow. I'm coming to realize just how important my mission could be in helping lift this negativity so that others may be free. I am eager to serve. Just not sure exactly how I'm going to do this.

May 2, 2019

I've been trying to read *The Urantia Book* the past few days. In general, it gives a mind-blowing detailed account of the complex nature of God, of governing intergalactic hierarchies, of the nature of the universe and beyond. It describes Urantia's (Earth's) history and evolution in great detail. Some of it makes my eyes cross. Jesus' life and teachings make up a large portion of its 2,000 pages. It's a massive amount of information.

The origination of the text is somewhat mysterious. Over the course of many years, the text came through an unnamed human source, possibly originating from other-worldly, higher-dimensional beings. At the end of each section, the being or entity who brought forth the material is described. For example, Paper 43 - The Constellations, attributes the content for that paper in this way: *[Sponsored by Malavatia Melchizedek.]* Paper 91 - The Evolution of Prayer is attributed like this: *[Presented by the Chief of the Urantia Midwayers.].*

Three of the four sections were complete in 1934. The fourth and final section on Jesus' life and teachings was delivered in 1935.[13]

The material, while fascinating and utterly comprehensive, hadn't seemed very relevant to what I'm trying to do now and my questions about Mother Earth and its previous inhabitants. Today I said aloud, "Please let me know if there is something in particular I need to be reading in this material, or I'll be done with it." I spent a few minutes looking over the lengthy table of contents, when it came to me to search for John the Baptist. Sure enough, there's a whole section dedicated to John.

It's a lovely account of his life, his preaching and his relationship with Jesus. As it came to his imprisonment and death, I couldn't help but cry, once again.

Here are bits of the story of John the Baptist from *The Urantia Book (*The Urantia Book, Part 4, Paper 135). I'm asking Metatron, when shall John and I again pick up where we left off on our shared story? I miss him dearly.

In a few passages of The Urantia Book concerning John the Baptist, John is described as being direct, to the point, a man of relatively few words… just as he had described himself to me on October 26, 2018. As an example:

> 135:4.5 It was the influence of Elijah that caused John to adopt his methods of direct and blunt assault upon the sins and vices of his contemporaries. He sought to dress like Elijah, and he endeavored to talk like Elijah; in every outward aspect he was like the olden prophet. He was just such a stalwart and picturesque child of nature, just such a fearless and daring preacher of righteousness. John was not illiterate, he did well know the Jewish sacred writings, but he was hardly cultured. He was a clear thinker, a powerful speaker, and a fiery denunciator. He was hardly an example to his age, but he was an eloquent rebuke.

Many passages explain the foundational beliefs of the time and the driving focus upon the coming "kingdom of heaven", a concept preached by both John and Jesus 2,000 years ago. I see the parallels between these teachings and what is happening now with the ascension. Has it just taken two millennia for this time to come?

> 135:5.8 It becomes apparent, therefore, that John's announcement of the coming kingdom had not less than half a dozen different meanings in the minds of those who listened to his impassioned preaching. But no matter what significance they attached to the phrases which John employed, each of these various groups of Jewish-kingdom expectants was intrigued by the proclamations of this sincere, enthusiastic, rough-and-ready preacher of righteousness and repentance, who so solemnly exhorted his hearers to "flee from the wrath to come."

> 135:6.8 … he counseled all: 'Make ready for the end of the age — the kingdom of heaven is at hand.'

Lovely and interesting accounting of John's baptizing of Jesus in the River Jordan on January 14, A.D. 26:

> 135:8.4 John had just begun baptizing the candidates for the day. Scores of repentants were standing in line awaiting their turn when Jesus and his two brothers took up their positions in this line of earnest men and women who had become believers in John's preaching of the coming kingdom. John had been inquiring about Jesus of Zebedee's sons. He had heard of Jesus' remarks concerning his preaching, and he was day by day expecting to see him arrive on the scene, but he had not expected to greet him in the line of baptismal candidates.

> 135:8.5 Being engrossed with the details of rapidly baptizing such a large number of converts, John did not look up to see Jesus until the Son of Man stood in his immediate presence. When John recognized Jesus, the ceremonies were halted for a moment while he greeted his cousin in the flesh and asked, "But why do you come down into the water to greet me?" And Jesus answered, "To be subject to your baptism." John replied: "But I have need to be baptized by you. Why do you come to me?" And Jesus whispered to John: "Bear with me now, for it becomes us to set this example for my brothers standing here with me, and that the people may know that my hour has come."

> 135:8.6 There was a tone of finality and authority in Jesus' voice. John was atremble with emotion as he made ready to baptize Jesus of Nazareth in the Jordan at noon on Monday, January 14, A.D. 26. Thus did John baptize Jesus and his two brothers James and Jude. And when John had baptized these three, he dismissed the others for the day, announcing that he would resume baptisms at noon the next day. As the people were departing, the four men still standing in the water heard a strange sound, and presently there appeared for a moment an apparition immediately over the head of Jesus, and they heard a voice saying, "This is my beloved Son in whom I am well pleased." A great change came over the countenance of Jesus and, coming up out

of the water in silence, he took leave of them, going toward the hills to the east. And no man saw Jesus again for forty days.

Today I walked the beach at sunrise then tried to spot the Great Horned Owl that lives in a grove of palm trees about a mile down the beach. Always I sit on the beach after the sun is up past the water line and ask for protection and say my prayers. Today I grabbed a grocery bag from home and picked up trash along the way. No owl.

After my morning walk, I scarfed down a piece of peanut butter on toast then walked down the street to a neighbor's house for some just-roasted, fresh-ground decaf coffee. Leaving there, I crossed paths with a man that I randomly met up on a hike a few days ago. On that hike, I was by myself and had taken a wrong turn somewhere. I was just realizing that I was lost when he came trotting down the path in front of me. He was quite a savior for me that day and got me going back on the trail I had meant to take, about ¾ of a mile back the way I came.

As he came down the road today, I instantly recognized him as the man from the hike. I said, "Hey, you are the guy that saved me on that hike a few days ago!" He recognized me. We shook hands and formally introduced ourselves this time. I will call him Greg. Greg was just out walking today, heading to the beach to check it out. Greg told me that his good friend just recently came across a five-foot rattlesnake, exactly where I was hiking the other day. The snake was sunning himself on the trail and, had he not rattled his rattle, the man may not have seen him at all. That could have been devastating. Greg recommended I stick to the wide fire roads and stay off the small mountain bike trails that wind all over the place in the nearby hills. I told him I'd be staying off that trail for good! I'll be sticking to the beach for my walks.

I've had several synchronicity moments while here in Baja, this just being one more to add! I am so grateful. I've even started to view every situation, everyone I meet, as part of a divine plan in the matrix. How do all the pieces fit together? What can I learn here from this situation or from this person? How can I be in my heart in this particular moment, be of service? Am I being presented with a challenge or opportunity? I do believe that nothing happens randomly, there is no such thing as coincidence.

It is so fun to have this opportunity to just completely go with the flow. Be led, instead of always taking the lead. Surrendering instead of planning.

This afternoon I joined 13 local neighborhood ladies (and one man) at the resort next door for lunch in the pool. I heard some great stories. Many of them live here in paradise full-time as retirees. One woman is a professional diver and offered to teach me how to dive. She talked about literally sitting on the ocean floor, silently observing. Letting the life come to her in all its beauty and delight. This reminded me of the channeling I did with Metatron, written in this journal on February 3rd, 2019, where he said, "Sit at the bottom of the ocean and let the gentle swaying of the water move you. You're not fighting it. You're not forcing it. You're not influencing it. You're simply going with the flow. And you start to feel Mother Earth below you, beneath you, around you and within you. And you become one with the water." I may give diving a try.

May 3, 2019

I heard last night to double my meditation time, eat less and drink lots of water.

Roger that.

Thinking more about John the Baptist today. Back on October 22nd, 2018, the day before I started this journal, Metatron reached out to me about John. I was so excited to start this journey with John, to be working with such an amazing figure in our history. That night, I felt tension in my jaw, so opened it up to see if anyone wanted to come through with a message. This is what I recorded that day, about four minutes long.

"Hi Shawna. This is Metatron. Yes, I'm smiling with you, too. We are overjoyed, I am overjoyed for you. I feel your giddiness, I feel your happiness. We all rejoice in these moments when these big leaps are taken, understanding has come to your awareness and things become more clear, and you step even more firmly into your purpose and into your divine self. It's just such a beautiful unfolding and we are all enjoying it along with you.

"You have a lot of eyes on you. You are so important to what's going on right now. And I know I've said it to you before, and I don't want you to feel that pressure to perform or be a certain way or do a certain thing at a certain time. You are doing your best and your best is more than good enough for what we have going on right now. We are thrilled with your progress. You should be very proud of yourself. In seven short weeks you have completely transformed yourself. You've done it with a smile, you've done it with grace, you've done it with love, you've done it with humility. You are truly an inspiration to those around you who are seeing this and feeling you. It's so very powerful.

"You will come to know your power and you've got a lot of love around you and people and entities helping you unleash that power in a controlled way, to feel that vibration, feel that resonance. There will be a time, I promise, where you will put that energy to good work. You'll do amazing things with that energy, especially when you pair up with your twin flame. This union with John is heavenly. You are in your reward life, Shawna. What a beautiful, sacred union. Savor this moment. Savor this time. You'll look back on this very fondly."

(My tears started to flow, and I whispered aloud, "Yes, I will. It is really incredible.")

"Oh, dear one. Let your emotions out. When you are able to cry you are able to make more room for other energies to come in and take its place. So, cry it out. Feel those emotions. Feel the depth of this. It is deep. It is your core. This is your core speaking, your core expressing itself. This is you remembering who you are."

(I'm crying pretty hard at that point. I said through my tears, "Yes. I had no idea. I didn't know. I feel like I am cheating or something, like I am not worthy of this. I have so much gratitude for you, Metatron." I took a few deep breaths. "Thank you, Metatron". To which he replied, *"You are welcome, get some rest."*)

It seems that the long-anticipated pairing with my twin flame could be only days away. So very close. Our deeper energy resonance has already started.

And my life shall never be the same.

Then, sometime after my twin flame and I unite, John the Baptist and I will come back together to finish our "epic" tale about our shared life together. It gives me a bit of anxiety to know we haven't finished this work yet. I always have to remind myself to surrender and have faith. All in perfect timing.

May 5, 2019

Deep emotions coming up today. Feels like it is because I'm about ready to take deeper steps into my transition, and I am grieving for the death of my old self.

Dying. Only to be born anew.

May 8, 2019

Very interesting several days. Ramirah's energy seems to be anchoring more fully into my energy system. I am also back to being able to see him more clearly and hear him again. The extra meditation is making a big difference. I'm so very happy and excited for this unfolding! I'm feeling a major full-body slow pulsation of energy that starts at my root and expands up into my heart area when I get quiet. Pulse. Pulse. Pulse. Maybe every three seconds. This is the first time I've felt this energy wave. So beautiful and loving and affirming. I sat in meditative joy for probably an hour today, just feeling into this and sending Ramirah love.

Leading up to this pulsing energy, I was again very emotional. Feeling disconnected from Ramirah's energy. Mourning my mom.

Lately I've been seeing a skeleton in a black robe behind me, with his bony skeleton hands resting lightly on my shoulders. I've grown pretty fond of him actually. Named him "Skeletron". I wonder if Metatron finds that amusing. Somehow, I find that unlikely! I think this character represents the dark and is foretelling of major changes coming up for me—death and of course rebirth. I've been wondering, where does my dark side fit into this ascension equation?

Yesterday I put it out to the Galactic Council that I'd like to start seeing some of the many amazing beings who are on the council. A few interesting visions have been popping into my head. Today as I laid in the sun on my beach towel, with the whole beach to myself, I asked if anyone wanted to come into my vision and let me see them. Oh boy! I didn't know what to expect but what happened was incredible! Ra said to let my imagination go crazy, so that is what I did. (And I asked for protection.)

A Praying Mantis-type being appeared first. Just the head, front and center in my mind's eye. I'm thinking this is likely just my imagination. I had recently seen a video where the galactic Mantid race was shown (basically a huge praying mantis). In the spirit of imagination, I just went with it.

I acknowledged it, said hello. It shook my hand with its insect-like hand. I told this being that it was amazing, what a sight! I thanked it for coming forward. The being then moved aside to show me a bunch of Mantids behind it—maybe 30 of them, all grouped together. I was not expecting that! I expressed my delight at seeing all of them, and I thanked them for letting me see them. Then they all started clapping for me, showing me respect and admiration. Then they took a small bow as a gesture of appreciation. I actually started crying as I watched this from my beach towel. So touching to feel that love and appreciation coming from these beings. I bowed back and told them thank you and I said that I loved them. Wow.

Several more beings came forward. Even if this was all just in my head, from my own ego or imagination, it was still amazing! (Don't ignore it, explore it!) I met a lion being with a huge fluffy mane. I couldn't help but want to put my fingers into that mane. I am sure that was completely inappropriate! Thank goodness these are abundantly loving beings! I met his female mate as well.

He was on four legs, but she was standing upright. I got the sense that they walk either on all fours or upright.

I then saw a blue female feline who was tall and regal. She reminded me of the blue beings in the movie *Avatar*. I met a few dinosaur-looking beings who had feathers coming out the tops of their heads. Tall with small upper bodies and large guts, large lower bodies. Maybe 12 feet tall. The first one starting licking me all the way up my body with a big pink tongue. It felt really nice actually! Then two more of them joined in. Those two scooped me up with their tongues to where my feet weren't touching the ground and the first one gave me what felt like a tongue massage. I know, crazy! Of course, I thanked them profusely for their kindness.

Next, a being came forward who seemed to be kind of crouching, tan colored with dark patterns and stripes on its body. It seemed female, about my size. I asked her if she was Reptilian and she said no. She came over to me and started whispering in my ear. I didn't hear anything but possibly my spirit heard her.

Then a gelatinous looking fellow came into view with a semi-transparent face whereby the eyes were set on each side of its head, its skin slightly-see through, white and pale yellow. He(?) did not have legs, but a round body that he scooted around in. I put my hand on his head to feel his skin, which was like cartilage. Again, likely a highly inappropriate thing to do, to touch him! Sheesh.

Next a white wispy being came into view with large dark eyes. It seemed to have several skinny arms and was kind of shy. It didn't really face me but looked to the side. The last being who came forward seemed to be somewhat amphibian with dark shiny skin, but I only really got a good look at its left eye. It was giving me a pretty intense stare. Mesmerizing really. I started to feel my energy flutter a bit, in a good way. It reminded me of the great eye in the *Lord of the Rings* movies. As the being stared into me, I got very quiet and just felt its presence.

Okay. Wow. I thought that was plenty for one sitting! Truly incredible. I'll do that again soon. I got up and took a dip in the sea.

May 11, 2019

Such peace, beauty, stillness yet vibrancy. Feeling the amazing support and love of the Galactic Council and Metatron, every day. I am so grateful. My vibration is humming along, flowing, swirling. Blissful, light. Almost two full months into this journey and still loving every minute of it. Life here is settling into a rhythm of restful sleep, sunrise meditations and prayers, connecting, communicating, channeling the Galactic Council and Metatron, guided meditations, sitting in mindful silence, preparing and eating vegan foods, socializing with my new-found friends, chatting with my husband, texting family, sun worshipping at the beach, floating and swimming in the sea. Writing in this journal. Reading, reading, reading… so much good stuff to read. Watching and listening to the birds all around me. Not one, but two Great Horned Owls this morning. Precious.

I asked Metatron yesterday if I'd continue to write the book with John the Baptist. He said eventually, but right now there are more important tasks at hand. He said, however, that I could connect with him whenever I'd like. Which I did this morning briefly.

I was sitting outside my yurt having just finished my bowl of cereal when a vision starting coming in.

I closed my eyes and took a couple deep breaths. Dirt floor, a wooden chair, white walls, low ceiling. A chunky wood table comes into my view. Then hands started to move all over my body from behind me. Up my sides, up my neck, into my hair, across my chest. Felt so good. Turned around to find John there, looking into my eyes. He kisses me deeply, and I kiss him back. So happy to see him. He gingerly removes his white linen robe which falls to the floor. Then he hoists me up on this big table and enters me swiftly. In and out, such pleasure. Scorching and hot in a matter of seconds. In and out. I lay back on the table with my arms stretched out on each side. I'm trying to see if I'm me in this body now, or if I'm the dark-skinned woman from our earlier encounters. Fuzzy, I'm perceiving both. Me thinking about this seems to cool things down for John and me. I sat back up and we kissed a bit more. I'm smiling into these kisses.

I'm still reading *The Urantia Book*. Getting into the materials on Jesus' life and teachings. Really captivating. According to this book, Jesus was given the opportunity to take advantage of angelic and other-worldly powers to help with his ministry, but he decided against it. He'd walk his path like an ordinary man which he felt was in alignment with the will of God, The Father. The book explains how Jesus was to set upon his journey, being fully a man but with a divine spiritual mission:

> Step by step this human mind follows in the path of the divine. The human mind still asks questions but unfailingly accepts the divine answers as final rulings in this combined life of living as a man in the world while all the time submitting unqualifiedly to the doing of the Father's eternal and divine will.[13]

Carla Rueckert, the woman who channeled all the *Ra: Law of One* material in the 70s and 80s has written a few books that help translate the *Law of One* material and provide practical guidance for everyday living and spiritual growth. In her book *Living the Law of One 101: The Choice,* Carla talks about living out our days in faith, with a surrendering to the divine. This spoke right to the core of me.

> The whole point of faith is that we choose to take the leap into faith with no outer proof. We leap because we embrace the mystery, the paradox and the state of the unknowing which characterize a life lived in faith. We let these qualities call us forth into the mid-air of unproven faith. And we find our feet in that very mid-air, and come into our faith organically, once we make the leap.[1]

Even with all this knowledge, all this love, all the support I feel on a daily basis, I am feeling very sad tonight. Crying and crying. The illusion is just so strong. I am bawling as I connect with Ramirah in my mind, in my heart and energy. It isn't enough. I want him all the way. I want him physically with me. I want our complete and utter coupling which transcends all human understanding.

He's with me in my mind, on his knees, comforting me with his love and sweet words. John, Jesus and Roykilva stand behind me with their hands on my back. The Mantid I met the other day is here as well, offering love and support. They seem to understand this Earthly third-density conundrum, this deep longing in my core to completely dissolve this veil of separation. It's like I've had a real taste of this oneness and this love with Ramirah, and now I want more, more, more. A part of me feels hopeless as though this will never fully happen.

Tonight, as I let these emotions run their course through my beingness, I sat outside and watched the sky darken and the stars light up. It was warm and calm outside and everything had a soft silver glow from the half-moon above. One particular star, somewhat lower on the horizon but aligned perfectly in front of me, caught my attention. It flickered and seemed to shimmy a bit. I watched it intently. The star seemed to disappear, then reappear instantly slightly to its left, then back again to its original position. About a minute later, it happened again. The star shifted to the left, then a bright white flash of light happened right above it! I couldn't believe it! Then above that flash, a few seconds later, another bright flash. Like a camera's flash going off. I felt all this love in my heart as this happened. Plus, my adrenaline kicked in. I take this to be a sign from my galactic friends above who are watching me and supporting me on this journey. What a delight. Again, I am so humbled.

May 12, 2019

Mother's Day. Again, I'm so emotional today. So hard knowing my mom is not of this earth any longer. I miss her dearly. This is harder than I thought it would be. I think I'm just raw right now. Need to get quiet, feel into my breath, crawl into my heart and just float for a while.

Last fall when I started doing the Metatron Merkaba meditation on a daily basis, and after I had learned of the existence of my twin flame, I cried a lot during one particular part of the meditation. In the sequence Metatron asks us to visualize coming together with our first love, the one that fulfills all our longings for love. We bring that love into our hearts then send that love up to our third eye. I'd feel this deeply and would cry most times I did this. I asked for either Metatron or the Galactic Council to explain to me why I cry during this part. Most of what was said (I believe this was the Galactic Council):

> "Shawna, please allow me some time to answer this for you. Your sadness is deep, it goes back many lifetimes. You've been preparing for your twin flame now for several lifetimes…Your soul knows about your twin flame, but your body, your mental, your emotional states in this physical form are unaware, have forgotten. But you still feel that lack. You feel that need. You feel that void.

> "This void has been filled by your spirit guide for many, many lifetimes. But it is also that you know when you reunite with your twin flame, that you can feel what that is truly like, to reunite with your other half; to feel that connection, to feel that love, to experience that bliss and have your energy open up. So you've had these relationships for many lifetimes, purposefully, that don't fulfill that inner soul's need. Because coming together with your twin flame will be so powerful. And you've known it is coming, have known for a while. This keeps you at a certain vibratory level on these Earth planes…

> "Know dear one, as you reunite with your twin flame, you will know love and completion that you've never experienced in this lifetime and many previous lifetimes. It will be glorious. It will be expansive. It'll be the truth. It will be so powerful. It must be powerful because what you two will be doing will require an immense amount of power. Immense amount of focus. It'll take both of your…energies combined to create a super energy that will help emancipate mankind. Free them from the binds of evil energy. This connection with your twin flame is so powerful, it will require…you living through God's will. Omnipotent, omnipresent, forever…stretching out to infinity. Your rapture will be never ending and always."

May 22, 2019

Just got back to Baja last night after spending five days up north for my son's graduation from college. This kid melts my heart every time. He is such an amazing, gentle, kind, loving soul. Pure goodness through and through. Huge amount of love in him, around him, flowing through him. I am so proud. And he is so happy to be done with school. He gets to experience the "death" of his college life and now his rebirth into a new major phase of being. It'll be great for my husband to have our son home; it won't be so lonely for him.

I am feeling so very good right now. Light, happy, balanced, content, peaceful, flowing.

May 25, 2019

More bright flashes of light in the night sky last night! Thank you, my galactic friends!

Two days before I left for home to see my son graduate from college, a new couple came to stay at the yurts. It was a spur-of-the-moment decision for them to be here. They thought they were staying in Loreto, Mexico, but alas, they didn't like beach scene there so drove down here to stay. I will call them Don and Selena.

Meeting these two was, again, divine synchronicity. Truly I'm feeling that just about everything that happens—the people I meet, the things I read, everything, is being divinely orchestrated on some level.

According to Don, he had been tortured and harassed by non-terrestrials living on Earth disguised as humans. The brunt of this torture happened in 2001. This experience lead to an attempted suicide and a three-month stint at a mental institution. Particularly in the past two years, he's completely gotten away from his spirit. His health has suffered greatly for it. I did some energy work on Don (calling forth Metatron to help, a method he described in *The Healing Book)*, and he did an amazing psychic reading for me. Just as important, we were able to be completely honest and open with each other about all the crazy shit that has been going on in our lives. We believe each other. We support each other. Selena, too. She's such a beautiful, sweet soul. We are emailing now and have become life-long friends. I have a feeling we'll need each other with how things are unfolding with this ascension.

Since Don and Selena left Spa Buena Vista and the yurts, Don says he's done a complete 180 on his spiritual life. Being here in this vibration and in this high frequency, I believe, helped Don raise his frequency level. Just as Metatron and the Galactic Council had said—my raised energy vibration will act as a tuning fork for others, raising their vibration if they are willing to accept it and embrace it. Resonance. I'm happy to think that I may have helped him get on a more positive path.

May 26, 2019

From The Urantia Book—Jesus' original preaching. I must be this little child.

> 137:8.8 Those who first seek to enter the kingdom, thus beginning to strive for a nobility of character like that of my Father, shall presently possess all else that is needful. But I say to you in all sincerity: Unless you seek entrance into the kingdom with the faith and trusting dependence of a little child, you shall in no wise gain admission.[13]

Tonight, I asked Metatron if I should be working toward publishing this journal while I'm down here. I asked if this material related directly to my mission. Through automatic writing, I captured this lovely response from him:

> *"This is a path you are on—an important path that, yes, others would find interesting and maybe even important and healing. But for now, your focus must be on your total and complete surrender to the awakening and unfolding happening in your beingness right now.*
>
> *"Quiet. Meditation. Inward. Absorbing. Letting it all flow in/out/all around. Don't get caught up in your headspace just now. Writing intently and intensely now will keep you in your intellect and distracted from your energy. It's about the energy flow my dear. This is all you need to be doing—in your bliss, staying clear and centered. Grounded. Opening yourself up to more and more possibilities. The places you will go my child—the realms you'll experience and the things you'll see. A true wonder, and we are all rejoicing to see and experience this with you on a very intimate level. Yes. We are right here, in your energy, experiencing your evolution, watching you, cheering you on.*
>
> *"So much love, my dear. You are just starting to fathom the love and support coming to you from your galactic and multidimensional family. You are home with us. You are our family. We are connected now very deeply. Your resonance has expanded beautifully, particularly as you approach each and every perceived challenge. You are doing so well. We applaud you my dear. So yes, the writing—you will know exactly what to do and the right time. We are guiding you at the most minute levels now. Helping in ways that you are not consciously aware of. Our reach is broad and deep my dear.*
>
> *"You are completely and utterly supported on this incredible journey of love, of light. Experience yourself in your true nature, as your true self. And the world will rejoice in what you can do."*

May 30, 2019

My depth of understanding, knowing and love has reached a new height! Feeling higher frequencies of unconditional love fill me up… more bliss, more shimmering energy, more love, love, love. Once again, I am drunk with this feeling. Such peace. Someone could drop me off in the middle of the ocean right now and I wouldn't have a care in the world. Just a smile on my face and a knowing that everything is going to be great.

It has been quite the ride the past few weeks to get to this point. There are things happening that I'm not quite ready to write about.

During my meditation today, I believe Metatron came in and told me that he'd like me to publicly channel him. That I need to await instructions. I'd be honored and delighted to serve in that way. I am all in! I got the impression that this won't be a YouTube thing, at least not initially. More of an event setting or group setting. I'm sure he'll make it completely clear when the time comes and the time is right to do this.

After this meditation, I sat basking in a sea of light. Feeling my energy ebb and flow just like the Sea of Cortez, as if I'm just floating on the surface. Expand, contract, expand, contract. It's a new feeling in my energy. Then I experienced myself as complete white light, seeing truly how the body is just a vehicle, a vibrating, energetic vehicle so that I can experience myself as an individuation of the Great Creator, of God. I may be understanding this on a mental level and even a bit of a feeling level, but today was different. It was all encompassing and just natural. I am so humbled by this experience. Thank you so much to Metatron, my higher self, my galactic friends, Ramirah, and of course anyone else who may not be in my conscious awareness but who is helping me, nonetheless.

May 31, 2019

The *Urantia Book* has a chapter entitled "The Ordination of the 12". This piqued my interest, as it sounds similar to *enlightenment of the 12* that I kept hearing on November 6, 2018 as captured in this journal. I just finished reading this chapter this morning.

This Urantia text is pretty incredible. Not only easy to read and understand, but provides more detail, context and nuance which don't seem to be included in The Bible (at least in my understanding). It's almost a day-by-day overview of Jesus' life and his teachings. Super comprehensive and totally interesting.

Briefly, this chapter explains how Jesus taught and related to the original 12 apostles. Those original messages are clearly articulated in the text. The text also explains how hard it was for these 12 apostles to really get what the heck Jesus was trying to say. They were described as common, ordinary men of Earth, the "salt of the Earth" as Jesus said. Even as they were about ready to embark on a public tour of preaching Jesus' and The Father's word, they had doubts. They asked for more time with Jesus to really try to understand and grasp the teachings before they went out on their own.[13]

A high-level overview of some of the teachings that Jesus asked his apostles to preach and to exhibit every day, as described in Paper 140:

- Our spiritual journeys are inward and start within us.

- The Kingdom of God is within us. This knowing and feeling relies on faith, personal belief.

- While we may not be able to control what is going on around us, we can in fact control our emotions and our responses and actions to those things.

- Our personal character and related actions in the world are the representations of our faith. This is an experiential path. We exhibit our faith by what we do.

- In relation to the current religious doctrine that often is phrased as "not" doing something in order to be devout, e.g. "Thou shalt not …", Jesus said that "the happy and effective person is motivated, not by fear of wrongdoing, but by love of right doing." "Strong characters are not derived from *not* doing wrong but rather from actually doing right. Fear and shame are unworthy motivations for living a spiritual life."

- He urged and exhibited both fatherly love and brotherly love to every human on Earth.

- Boys and men should be tenderhearted and have empathy, just as women do. "Sympathy is a worthy attribute of the male as well as the female. It is not necessary to be calloused in order to be manly." "Being sensitive and responsive to human need creates genuine and lasting happiness, while such kindly attitudes safeguard the soul from the destructive influences of anger, hate and suspicion."

- No "eye for an eye" or "tooth for a tooth". Jesus said we should return good for evil. Be gentle toward all. Mercy should determine your love and your conduct.

- Seek to live without grudges and without vengeance. Jesus supported civil laws that punish evil-doers and crime. But he admonished the practice of personal retaliation. A wrong is not righted by revenge.

- Love your enemies.

- Have faith in the eventual triumph of divine justice and eternal goodness.

- Judge not, that you be not judged.

- Material possessions and abundance are fine; however, happiness does not come from these things. "What shall it profit a man if he gain the whole world and lose his own soul?"

- Jesus came to Earth to create in humanity a new spirit, a new will; to impart a new capacity for knowing the truth, experiencing compassion, and choosing goodness. The will that is in harmony with God's will.

- Love and the attributes of truth, beauty and goodness are the divine ideal and should be our eternal reality.

- Quoted directly from the book with sub-bullets added: John asked Jesus, "Master, what is the kingdom of heaven?" And Jesus answered: "The kingdom of heaven consists in these three essentials:

  ○ first, recognition of the fact of the sovereignty of God;

  ○ second, belief in the truth of sonship with God;

  ○ and third, faith in the effectiveness of the supreme human desire to do the will of God—to be like God. And this is the good news of the gospel: that by faith every mortal may have all these essentials of salvation."

June 7, 2019

Feeling SO MUCH BLISS. What Metatron and the Galactic Council told me last year is coming true. Just able to be in bliss all the time. I'll have more bliss than I can imagine. It's happening. I love it so much. THANK YOU.

Want to stay out of my head and just let this energy flow and allow this vibration to anchor into my beingness and elevate higher and higher. Reading Paul Selig's channeled books now, so amazing and of course perfect for where I'm at right in this moment. THANK YOU. I am in love. I am in love. I am in love.

June 18, 2019

I've been binge-reading Paul Selig's channeled books the past couple weeks. LOVE THIS material. Paul channels the Melchizedek—a group of highly evolved beings, a priesthood of sorts, from higher dimensions. *The Urantia Book* describes Melchizedek's services to Earth throughout history as well. I love how they speak and articulate their messages through Paul.

I was about 20 pages into the first book, *I Am the Word*, when I felt my energy vibration change. This group reached out to me telepathically to welcome me to the material and wish me lots of love. I was on an airplane at the time. This has happened to me several times now, whereby the entity being channeled makes a connection with me when I start reading their material. Metatron, Galactic Council, Jesus, Heru (Horus), Ra and now Melchizedek. I know this sounds crazy, and I get it. Then it happens to you, and it's not crazy anymore, its extraordinary. I am humbled.

My connection with the Melchizedek has grown stronger and stronger as I make my way through their messages, exercises and energy frequencies that come through their written words. Yes, just like the Metatron and Galactic Council books channeled by Robbie Mackenzie, these books also carry a palpable frequency that is undeniable. Deep, powerful, loving, transformational.

Today I personally channeled the Melchizedek and recorded this on my phone. I felt a tension in my jaw and knew they wanted to connect. Their surprising and enlightening message for me, which lasted about 10 minutes (audio recorded):

> *"Thank you so much for taking the time to speak with us right now.*
> *"As you know we are entering a new era. Things are really heating up. You are on the forefront of this ascension of humankind. You are leading the way here, you and many others. Bringing light, bringing peace and calm, bringing love. We see you as a great wave, the first great wave pushing into shore, clearing out the debris, picking up debris as you go, picking up people and new souls and energy and power. This thing is building and swelling and growing. You can see how, Shawna, as you get more and more momentum here the power just increases exponentially. Until everything has been devoured by this power.*
> *"So that is where you are my dear, you are at the front of this wave pushing forward. It is the hardest part. It is the hardest part.*
> *"This is not the time to be second guessing or to be scared. It's the time for knowing. The time for forward movement, clarity of thought. Commitment to mission. These are important times. You are very important to the ascension of humanity my dear. You see that we are here, we hold your hands, we look into your eyes and bless you with everything we have.*
> *"You are truly special to us. We look upon you as a loving mother would look upon a child. The potential, the beauty, the strength. You are coming into this knowing. You are there now on some level. Let us talk through this for a while my dear.*
> *"Not everything is as it seems.*

"There really is true evil on this planet. You know that intuitively, though you have not succumbed to this evil as most people have. You really do have a gift in where this kind of evil tends to wash around you as water would wash around a rock. But things are changing and the technology is getting smarter. As we've said, things are heating up, things are speeding up and getting a little more intense.

"This truly is the time to be careful and take heed and listen. To follow your guidance and be in touch with all of us who are doing what we can on the other side to help all of you with your feet on the ground. But again, you are in choice and you are in embodiment. And truly this will be led by you humans who have chosen this path—have chosen this path previously to be in that first wave, to knock down the barriers, to clear out the debris and leave a beautiful, pristine, clean environment after your wake.

"What you are doing is important. It's time to be focused as much as possible. Embrace your gifts. Bring that light in like a lighthouse. Let it shine, let it shine, let it shine.

"Use us as the power of your lightbulb. Let us illuminate that path. You just need to trudge forward confidently. We will illuminate that path so that you cannot miss it. Yes, continue to ask for protection. Get all those chess pieces all lined up where we need them so that you can move onto victory, easily and seamlessly.

"There are tough times ahead, my dear." (My tears start flowing as I feel into the words, as the words resonate with my knowing.)

"Yes, and you know that. As we've said, this will not be easy and there'll be times of sorrow…and stress. There'll be times of uncertainty and extremely hard decisions. But you are answering the Clarion Call my dear.

"This is your path; this is your destiny. And you will be successful. There'll come a time where you'll need to be laser focused. So, we're doing what we can to set the environment and the stage to allow that unfolding and allow that focus. And to allow you to completely synch into this life. We're helping you lay down the foundation for this change in your world, to allow this to happen. Going to make this as comfortable as possible for you my dear.

"You need only hear our voices, lead with your heart, and have complete faith and trust that this is the right way to go.

"Yes, keep praying for protection. Keep that protection in place. That is a vibrational frequency that's important and everybody who is on that path, we are asking everybody to do this at this time. There are real dangers there. We see you only as beauty…true beauty manifest. Even with the pain and the sorrow, the hurt, the anger and guilt, you are perfect in God's eyes.

"We leave you with this. Now is the time for focus. Now is the time for the Clarion Call. The call you have answered. The life that you have chosen is in full motion. Hear the roar of this water, of this wave, as it pushes through, pushes through and makes a path to enlightenment. Whereby people will be able to follow you. Energies will be able to follow you, resonate with you, and propel you even further. You may get some bumps and bruises on the way, but we promise you my child, this will all be worth it. What you're doing is important.

"There'll be no mistaking the plans, the communications and the steps you need to take. We leave you in love my child."

Thank you so much Melchizedek. I love you so much.

With my free will, I give myself over to Divine Will. I make room for my higher self to become who I am in every moment. I pray to continue to hear your words, your guidance, clearly. And to have the energy, strength and power to act upon that guidance. To continue to step fully into my mission. I am happy to be of service.

Planning another trip home for my Mom's Celebration of Life, happening around her birthday on June 23rd. Will be home for about a week.

July 3, 2019

I am basking in the serene beauty of the Sea of Cortez. I will never tire of this place. It's getting nice and hot outside, morning 'til night. The sea is a beautiful clear pool of warm, turquoise heaven. I'm swimming every day. Meditating in the water. Exercising in the water. Just soaking it up and thanking it for how amazing it is. I love it so much. A part of me will be floating in this water for eternity.

My skin is a rich bronze tone and my hair has bleached out on the ends. I feel beautiful inside and out.

Three and a half months into my Sea of Cortez sojourn. I'm spending a good two-to-three hours most days reading Paul Selig's books and doing the exercises they recommend. Listing all the things that keep me in fear. Listing all the ways I don't feel I'm free. In the books we are floating down rivers and climbing mountains. Walking up imaginary steps and opening imaginary doors to our truth. We are entering the Upper Classroom where lies cannot exist. The material is incredible and deep and is helping me figure out who I am and why I'm here. Who we ALL are and what we are ALL doing here. Throughout the texts they refer to creating the world anew in a higher octave—which in my mind is referring to this current ascension.

I'm developing my personal relationship with the Melchizedek more and more. I am continuing to deepen my connection to Ramirah and my higher self, maintaining my high vibration and consciously emanating love from my heart chakra. I still have moments of self-doubt and feelings of unworthiness.

After yesterday's meditation, a man came into view in my mind's eye. Glasses, heavy-set. He said his name was Ivan. I recognized him somehow, maybe from my dreams. Ivan told me that the alien technologies that are meant to slow down this ascension have gotten very powerful. He said they can cause a full coma on one end of the spectrum, to just being tired all the time on the other end. He said that my support team (beings of the light) have technologies to counteract these weapons, and that he needed my permission to use them on me. I hesitated a bit not knowing for sure if he was on the good team but decided it would be okay to trust him since I had been praying for protection so much. My team wouldn't let him through if he wasn't of the light. I told him yes. I haven't felt any difference yet.

I had a tough but impactful call with my husband two nights ago. He was trying to tell me that the past two months were the worst times of his life with me being gone. As he spoke, I felt the warm loving energy of my guides holding space for me. I spoke my truth with gentleness and love—but I was firm. He is building the brewery of his dreams and has been completely excited about that. Plus, I had been home twice in the past two months. I reiterated how important this trip was to me, and how good it has been for me and my journey. I was able to get him back on a positive track. He came around and admitted that what he said wasn't really true.

July 9, 2019

I came across a great book by Steve Nobel, *Personal Transitions: Beyond the Comfortable Into the Real*. I had seen Steve's meditations all over YouTube and had done a few of them, very powerful. I felt drawn to this book as I know that I am going through a massive transition.

More introspection on what I really want in life. What are my wildest dreams? For now I am focusing on my mission and maintaining my high vibration. I'm already in an environment that is my heaven on Earth. I am in my bliss. Wishing I was closer to Ramirah. I am still not consciously emancipating Reptilian energy, nor do I know how to do this. What can I be doing to move this along?

I am starting to ask my support team about my time here in Mexico. It's getting hot. Hurricane season is around the corner. I don't have air conditioning in my yurt, so I am contemplating moving locations. My plan was to be here for six months, which puts me into mid-September. I'll have to have air conditioning and safety against hurricanes if I'm going to make that work.

And what about when I return home? What then? I have no idea.

July 19, 2019

I've often visualized myself in a deep, dark cave, sitting cross-legged, where my galactic team and Metatron send me souls for healing work. I am seeing this again as I look through a neighbor's book on cave paintings spread through central Baja. I am getting a strange energy fluctuation as I see these ancient and mysterious paintings on the pages. Many of the figures look alien as if they are wearing space suits. I would love to see these in person. Can I make that happen? I sketched some of the cave drawings in a notebook.

Feeling introspective again tonight.

Who am I without my earthly frame of reference?

Is it meaningful to even ask questions like this?

What does it matter? This is all an illusion.

We decided to incarnate on this earth for specific reasons. We have lessons to learn. Our soul yearns to evolve. We are 100% responsible for everything happening in our lives. We are in choice and in accord with everything going on—the good, the bad and the ugly. We have ultimate control. This dense plane of existence is a grand theater and we are the lead actors. This is our stage, our show, our reality that we are creating every day through our choices, beliefs, decisions and actions. Choose wisely and with love! MAKE IT COUNT.

July 20, 2019

It's the one-year anniversary of my mom's death. Mom, I love you with all my heart and I appreciate everything you gave to me and to this world. I know you are happy and thriving on the other side. I know you are supporting me and loving me and helping me along my path. Our song, "You're My Best Friend" by Queen…I see us arm in arm, laughing and singing this to each other.

July 21, 2019

Another exercise in one of Paul Selig's books, *The Book of Mastery: The Master Trilogy Book 1*. What do I need now? What do I need to grow?

The answer came. I have spent most of my life taking care of others and putting them first. Now it is time for me to put me first. Take care of me.

My support team assures me that I'll have all the abundance I need. I should not have any worries right now. Go with the flow. Keep my vibration up. Yes, feel into my emotions, then use my tools to work through them.

In my meditation this afternoon, I clearly connected with my lovely support team, even Micah! I hadn't seen Micah in months. I was so happy to see him. It was a brief hello and hug.

Roykilva said that things are going well, but tough. The Reptilians are doing everything they can to stop this ascension. They will not accept defeat. My mission is important. I need to be in embodiment here on Earth to do this work. Critical. It'll be a life-long mission. Get settled in for the long ride.

John the Baptist came into view with a huge hug. I told him that I felt bad that we never finished our book. He said the stories are already in our hearts, in our heads and in our throat chakras. I started to cry. He said the stories will come out all in good timing. I asked about the baby—all in good time he repeated.

Jesus came next and lit up my halo he gifted me several months ago. He then kissed me on the forehead. Lovely.

Metatron visited last—his giant presence enveloping me. I looked at the clock and it said 11:11! He embraced me from behind and we spun in my Merkaba for a few minutes. Felt expansive and loving.

I am so humbled by this group and all their love and protection. Thank you, my team.

July 27, 2019

I am again praying for help and guidance on what to do with my remaining time here in Baja. The heat at night in my yurt is kind of unbearable. I need air conditioning and safety in case a hurricane or two decide to blow in.

What do I want to manifest for myself? What would make my heart sing? I know I am not ready to be home permanently. I'll be coming home in early August for a family reunion camping trip. Want to come back here to Mexico afterward.

My amazing team had this to say, hand-written in my journal:

> *"Shawna, if I may, thank you. We are so honored to help you at this juncture. So many considerations, yes? We would say follow your heart on this one. Get in touch with your heart-mind. What is it saying? You are on the right path. Where you are, per se, isn't the most critical part of your journey, it is how you are being. But that being said, you are in a perfect place to nurture your soul, bring balance and clarity to who you really are. Are you 'done' with this process? No. Not likely ever done with it. That is okay. Your life's journey and experience are all there is for you on this plane. It is why you've come here in the first place."*

Okay, thank you so much!

I am going to sketch out a rough plan for the remainder of my time here—letting my excitement be my guide. I am excited but a part of me is sad knowing that this experience will be coming to an end soon. (I have to come back to the States eventually; my passport is expiring soon!)

August 5, 2019

Freedom. I need freedom to step fully into my mission, into the next phase of my journey. I will know. Have faith. Patience.

I will know…okay. But I'm having massive bouts of anxiety. What does this mean and how will I know? This type-A overachiever, project manager-type is STILL uncomfortable with not knowing how something is going to end up. Even after everything that has happened to me, after all the incredible messages and support! Sheesh!

Going to rent a car and take a three-week tour of southern Baja by myself after I get back from this family reunion in Eastern Washington. It's going to be EPIC. My own personalized Baja beach tour.

My dad and my husband said they are super worried about me doing this by myself in Mexico. Everyone I've spoken to here locally says it should be safe and to go for it. YES, PLEASE AND THANK YOU.

August 7, 2019

I trust my support team 100%.

I know myself in truth.

My vibration is a beacon for others.

I am on my path. Firmly.

My next steps will be abundantly clear. I just need to follow the path illuminated before me. Trust in love.

Visual of a boat. I've been living on this boat for many years. I've grown very fond and accustomed to this boat. I've let go of the idea that there's a huge, amazing world out there. I haven't realized that I've become tethered to this boat. I can't be tethered and also do all the things I want to do in this life. I must move on from the boat. Set out. Wander. Explore. Touch and be touched. Expand and help expand.

Trust.   Patience.   Surrender.   Faith.

My mind, my heart and my actions need to be in alignment.

August 9, 2019

I've left the yurts and Spa Buena Vista behind, my home for the past four and a half months. I'm now in La Ventana, BCS, Mexico. Small town, super quiet now that it is off-season. For six months out of the year this town packs up with kite boarders starting in October. Right now it's pretty dead around here. I'm spending a lot of time in meditation. I'm staying on the beach in a great little casita—with AC! The sea water is a bit murky with seaweed. Not as pristine as Spa Buena Vista.

Going fishing on a small panga boat with people that I met here. Hoping to catch SOMETHING. Will release it of course! Enjoying the change of scenery and the few people I'm meeting. Walked about a mile down the beach today to have dinner. Lovely evening but super humid. You just get used to having a sweaty upper lip at all times when outside and not in air conditioning!

(I ended up catching a huge Rooster Fish on the fishing trip! What an experience. Could have been about 90 pounds. It put up a good fight, poor thing. We released it without any issues. It swam away in a hurry.)

August 15, 2019

I've rented a car and am in Todos Santos for a few nights. I'm loving it here so far! Art, cobblestone streets, amazing restaurants. Super nice people. The drive out here was easy, no issues. I'm visiting the local beaches which are on the Pacific Ocean on the west side of the Baja peninsula. I'm kind of scared of the bigger waves. Plus, I might lose my bathing suit top!

La Paz will be my next stop for a couple nights. Then I'll drive north to Loreto for a few nights, then end with a bang in Mulegé (moo-leh-HAY) for a week. Mulegé is supposed to have incredible beaches. I'll come home after that, end of this month. Timing should be about right; I expect to be ready to be home.

I've been pretty busy the past few days. I reached out to the Galactic Council and asked how long I should be meditating at this stage of my evolution, and at this phase of my Baja adventure. What would be optimal? Their response as I wrote it down in my journal:

"There is no set rule here my dear. What's most important is that you are always feeling connected and conscious of your energy frequency. Play with this idea. Bring it into your everyday state of being. Being truly connected to yourself in this way keeps you true to yourself. Brings the knowing of who you are and where you're at to the forefront of your consciousness. Stay connected to your heart at all times. Be in your heart space. Radiate from there. Feel it tingle and sparkle as the energy frequency is beamed out to all around you, to the cosmos.

"Feels blissful, yes? Here your mind gets a rest and your heart jumps for joy because it gets to be in the driver's seat. Cartwheels. Handstands. You'll feel lighter on your steps, lighter in your body, as your waves of bliss emanate out from you in all directions. You are doing it, Shawna. You are raising your frequency and doing God's work. You have no idea of the impacts you are already making on this plane."

(I thought, no I don't. I am just following my bliss, having fun.)

"Yes, my child this is how you are doing this. Look at your awareness of all the possibilities. Feeling into all the ways you can let go and be free. Do you see how important this work is? Vital. My dear. Never doubt this. What you are doing is important—even if it feels at times you are 'just playing'. This is all part of the plan. Freedom, playfulness, passion, surrender. Breathe. Cleanse. So yes, our recommendation would be for you to periodically get heart centered. Always be aware of your vibration, buzzing just under the surface. Take time for this and make it a priority. Yes, look for ways to adjust—what impacts that rate, either up or down? Then take action to maintain it at your highest levels."

(I thought, thank you! What about me crying and being sad about this transition? I shouldn't be sad; I should be happy all the time.)

"Should or shouldn't…catch yourself using these words; often this is the small self. Of course, if emotions come up for you it is important to experience them fully. Now you can take a moment to see your situation from the higher realms. See it from a broader, more informed and expansive perspective. This helps you process that emotion and move

on. If you leave a lot of those 'unpacked bags' in the room, the room gets awful crowded. The release of those emotions clears out those bags and makes room for new emotions and energies to be known. You are doing well."

I continued with my questioning. I asked if there was anything they can say or want to say in regard to where my mission will take me upon returning home in two weeks. I admitted that this was my fear talking. They answered:

"It's important that you don't know what the next steps may be at this time. You'll know when you'll know. This divine timing and unveiling is important to this unfolding, my dear. Continue to live in the moment and completely surrender to the guidance that will surely be there exactly when it needs to be." (Thank you!)

August 17, 2019

Arrived in La Paz today. Nice drive, no issues. Staying at a hotel on the marina. AC!

I feel so amazing. Glowing. Humming with love. Just having fun. Trying to notice when my energy is off (eating too much, thinking about my friend Monica). Also trying to let my heart lead. Easy to do that now, while I'm here in Mexico.

During my meditation today, my energy started going really deep. A forceful pressure started to grow on the back of my head. The vibration did not feel familiar, and I started to get a bit alarmed. I immediately asked my team for protection in case this was something negative.

I decided to visualize my Merkaba spinning around me. The energy did level out a bit. I began to see in my mind's eye an angel sitting on the bed with me. This angel was female and looked a lot like the actress Tilda Swinton! Tilda Swinton played the role of Archangel Gabriel, who was androgynous, in the film *Constantine*. Even though I had watched that movie years ago, that character had left an impression on me. I remember thinking how eerie she was in that movie. This angel told me that I was also an angel, that we are family. She said I was fully protected by my angel family. Brethren. Seraphim.

She said it was good that I ask for protection, but I should know it is always there. I asked her about these strange energy fluctuations. After a bit of a pause, she said that they are clearing out old/unneeded energies. I felt that clearing for a long time and my energy just seemed to go deeper and deeper.

Eventually I had more visions which are a bit fuzzy for me now. Trying to capture what happened while I can still remember.

First a voice told me that I was massively creative right now and I need to be careful about what I manifest. In fact, this voice said I should consciously try to be neutral for the time being. I need to be careful what I wish for, be careful where I put my focus and intention.

Then Ramirah appeared. He told me he was with me every minute of every day. Wow. Okay. I just need to know this for now…accept it as fact. It's okay if I don't fully understand it with my mind. Just KNOW. I saw visions of our thoughts merging as one. How do I know this is real? He looked deep into my eyes with this—his vertical black pupils set against a bright amber iris. Intense.

He said soon our thoughts will be inseparable, he reminded me. I remember kind of floating in a blissful dance with him for a while. He then said that his super masculinity helps neutralize MY masculinity and allows me to be more feminine—soft, nurturing, creative. Pure, sweet love. He is protecting me so that I can be completely vulnerable and surrender to love. How beautiful is that? I can lay down my armor. Stop being hard around the edges. I've come so far in this regard, but I know I can let all that armor go 100 percent. Be feminine, embrace this. Thank you, my love!

August 20, 2019

"Mantid" came into my awareness again today. This is the being from the large praying mantis-type race I had envisioned on May 8th. It seemed as though he kissed my hand. So sweet. He said he just wanted to tell me that I am doing great, fantastic, wonderful. To just relax. I told him that he sounds just like my ego. (I started to question if this was just my imagination or a real encounter.) He said that normally I am insecure about what I'm doing and how I'm doing it, which is true. I have a pretty big fear of failure. He said this was his way of counter-acting my insecurities. He put his left "hand" on my back and his right "hand" over my heart and again he told me to relax. He said I have an amazing support team and he'd like to be part of it. I told him, absolutely yes, I'd love that.

I am honored and humbled, once again.

Arrived in Loreto today. La Paz was amazing. The beautiful beaches and brilliant crystal-clear water there took my breath away. I had no idea that city had beaches like that. Every day it reached 100° but the Sea of Cortez was surprising cool in that area. Even the shallow bays were refreshingly chilly compared to Spa Buena Vista.

August 21, 2019

- I release all feelings of need around accomplishing something during this experience.
- I release all fear and worry about talking about my experience here.
- I release all fear about adjusting back into my former life (into my new life).
- I release all fear about the future.
- I release all fear about money.
- I am a beacon of light and hope for others.
- I see the divinity in all people, in all I see before me.
- My support team has my back—unconditionally.
- I experience myself as divine.
- I know myself as divine.
- This is the dawn of a new day. I embrace this day with all facets of my being.
- I operate from my heart space. I see all through the lens of love.
- By my witnessing of others in love, they are transformed.
- My softness is my gift. Radiate out softness.
- Give love freely. Accept love freely.
- Make time for me.
- Give and receive pleasure.

I was telepathically talking with the Melchizedek this afternoon while reading. One of the books, *The Book of Truth*, gives an example of a woman who is in a relationship where her needs are provided for. She doesn't need to work, she has dinner on the table every night for her children and husband, she cleans up after them. One day she realizes her fear of independence and self-governance has created her situation. She now sees her worth and wants to make a change that reflects her new truth.[14] I asked in my mind as I read this—what the hell does she do now? Assuming she doesn't stuff away her truth and fall right back into her routine?

The guides came in with a big answer. I saw a tall, rocky, scraggly mountain with bits of snow and ice at the top. The size of the mountain and its terrain would make it super hard to climb. At the same time, I sense the smell of the fresh mountain air. I see blue sky. I feel energized by the prospect of climbing that mountain. I don't have to run up the mountain. I can take my time. Enjoy the scenery, the fresh air, the sunshine…the birds and the critters. Take it one step at a time and enjoy the exercise, the oxygen in my lungs. Yes! I feel that. Then the guides came in and said they'd be with me the whole way. Loads of people, entities, support. Behind me. Each side of me.

Even in front of me. But I must be the one to walk, to make the journey. They won't fly me up there or carry me. I must make the journey on my own two legs.

There'll be mules carrying all the supplies. They'll provide me with all the tools and will show me how to use them. They'll enjoy the expansive vistas with me. Gaze at the stars with me. (I started to cry at these visuals.) And when I make it to the top, they'll celebrate my triumph with me. Such joy! Such an accomplishment. They said, Shawna my dear, you need complete freedom to do what you need to do. Spread your wings and soar. I asked about hurting my husband and my family. This was a fairly lengthy conversation, but to summarize, they said this will be a growth opportunity for my husband as well. As I see my situation and mission in truth, so will he. My letting go will help him let go—where he can be independent as well. No more crutch. This can all be done in love and in truth.

Just letting this sink in. Sigh.

August 22, 2019

Leaving Loreto today for Mulegé. My last week.

I am so happy I am able to have this experience. Thank you to my husband, my boys, my dad for your support, and thank you my entire support team for all you did to help me get here. I feel so amazing. Open, flowing, vulnerable, feeling my emotions deeply. Beginning to see more of the truth. I am dedicated to my mission.

I have NO PLAN. I surrender to the flow of my life as it unfolds moment to moment. Staying present and (trying to stay) in the now.

August 23, 2019

BEACHES. Beautiful, pristine, turquoise, clear water and amazing, white beaches. I. LOVE. THIS. SO. MUCH. Playa Armenta, Playa Requeson and Playa La Escondida, in just two days. So many beaches around Mulegé, so little time. I am in the off-season, so the beaches are pretty empty.

Mulegé is a small town near the mouth of the Río de Santa Rosalía, about half-way up the Baja peninsula on the east side. They call this an oasis town since it has a fresh water source with this river that runs through the middle of it. The town is full of lush greenery and palm trees which is in stark contrast to the rocky hills surrounding it. Most of the area's best beaches are south of town, within Bahia Concepcion (Conception Bay). There looks to be about a dozen beaches and I'm going to try to visit all of them before I'm done here. The beaches here are very different from those down south in Los Barriles and Spa Buena Vista. Instead of big expanses of sand, you have small inlets with sand that consists mostly of crushed seashells. Most of the beaches here also have small palapas for shade and overnight camping.

Besides the amazing beaches, this place also has ancient cave paintings nearby. This is a big one on my list of things to do while I'm here.

August 26, 2019

WOW. Felt another major energy update this afternoon, about an hour ago. Lots of activity happening as I wrap up this trip.

I was getting ready to buy the next Paul Selig book on Amazon.com when a small energy blast came in. It has been a while since I felt this energy. Felt so good. It subsided a bit, so I went back to what I was doing on Amazon. Whoosh! Here is comes back again, this time deeper. I went very deep. I closed my eyes and relaxed into it, breathing slowly. I thought, is this Ramirah?

The details are a bit fuzzy now, but I recall seeing the crystal skull that was energetically implanted in my throat several months ago light up. Then came in Ramirah with his matching skull, in front of me. These skulls began to merge in my mind's eye and started spinning as one unit. I could see light and darkness, and my energy was fluctuating. A voice came through and said, can you hear me? Yes, I said. The voice said that this was a gift—this is the truth—this is a NEW truth for me like I've never experienced it. A few minutes passed. Then it continued to say that this is very powerful. I must only use this for good, repeating that statement three times. Okay, my new truth.

This voice also said that the entire reason I'm on this planet now is to carry out my mission. EVERYTHING ELSE is simply an illusion.

I then pictured myself merging with Ramirah, front to front. My physical body as energy floated into his body, aligned head to head, throat to throat. My energy went crazy.

Ramirah told me not to be afraid. He is here with me always. The other voice came in and said to call upon them at any time. Any time. I sat in this new energy field, merged with Ramirah for about 20 minutes. I was so ecstatic to get to this milestone. Rejoicing inside! Ramirah, however, was mostly quiet, seemed almost reflective.

When I opened my eyes, the dining room looked "alive" and felt "alive". Alive in vibration, moving particles, dancing. As my gaze came back to my laptop screen with Amazon.com pulled up, I felt how powerful it was. Not the computer, but Amazon itself, as an entity. So powerful, almost hypnotic. Wow.

Thank you, team! Ramirah I love you so much. I am so honored and excited for this next phase, with you…beginning to merge into oneness.

I said a prayer and set an intention to anchor in the frequency permanently. I also envisioned Ramirah and I sending this love and light around the entire planet.

Took a guided tour of the cave paintings in Trinidad Canyon yesterday. We walked through the desert full of Cardon cactus, up dry riverbeds, around rocky cliffs and into shallow crevices where the paintings are visible. Beautiful scenery, great exercise, fascinating ancient artwork. I want to come back someday and go deeper inland to see more.

August 27, 2019

All the texts I've read lately from different authors and sources have similar lessons and themes. One of the most important concepts is the idea of resonance. Our energetic vibration impacts and effects all energy vibration rates around us. Your body, your beingness, your light, emits a frequency that other people feel on an energetic level. Everything is energy, everything has a vibrational rate, and these vibrational rates are interacting all the time.

As an example, if you have two tuning forks of the same frequency, striking one tuning fork will make the other one start to vibrate at the same rate. They will be in resonance with each other.

For those of us lightworkers who are being called to help with this ascension, this concept of resonance is key to the successful awakening of as many people as possible on Earth right now. From Metatron to the Galactic Council to Melchizedek, one of the most important things we can do right now is raise our personal vibration. This is critical.

Tonight, I had an energetic encounter with a new being as I sat on the couch, reading. My energy frequency picked up and I heard a voice, "Shaaaaaawnnnnaaaa"... I said, "Yes?" with a smile on my face. I got the impression that someone was doing a "show and tell" with me. A masculine entity was addressing others besides myself, and I heard something like, "She is aware I'm here, but settling into this energy frequency. She is a willing participant here." I was being observed. I said, "Yes, yes I am!" to that statement.

Then the entity addressed me directly. He said he was delighted to see me, be working with me. I felt that love and that delight to my core. I felt the respect and unconditional love. He asked how he made me feel. He said I should strive to see everyone on this plane in the same way—as divine perfection. Reverence. We talked about how my body and my energy will emit this frequency that they'll feel on multiple levels. Make this the goal. Exude this reverence, love, respect and delight to all I come into contact with. YES! Okay I will give it my best. Thank you!

August 28, 2019

My last full day in Mulegé! In Baja! Five and a half months in paradise.

One of the best ways to raise your vibration is to do what you are passionate about. What have I always loved, no question about it? Turquoise ocean water. White sand. Sunshine. These are my passions. What am I doing here, really? Raising my vibration, DUH! Metatron always says, follow your bliss. Do what gets you completely excited. This is your soul's way of pointing you in the right direction, toward your soul's mission here on Earth. Always do what brings you the most joy, happiness, excitement and bliss. This seems so obvious, but why is it so hard to do?

This trip to Baja has been a true gift. And I'm seeing how this is just the beginning of my new life.

I've experienced FREEDOM.

I've experienced FEARLESSNESS.

I've experienced STUNNING BEAUTY.

I'm beginning to experience myself in a new way. I am claiming my truth. My worth.

I'm seeing the world through my heart. I'm experiencing others around me as divine beings of light.

I'm beginning to see through the illusion and into the truth of who and what we really are. I AM FREE. I AM LOVE. WE ARE ONE.

I am here to help usher in a new reality here on Earth. To serve my fellow humans in the best way that I know how. I'm learning more every day.

With my free will, I surrender to Divine Will. I am your avatar in service. I am grateful. I am humbled.

DRAWING THIS PART OF MY JOURNEY TO A CLOSE

I'm back in the States from Mexico now for three months. I'm still processing, still integrating everything I've learned and experienced. I'm still coming to terms with my own personal transition as I step fully into my mission. Honestly, it hasn't been easy. I've been focused on publishing this book, at the urging of my higher self and my guides, for several weeks now. It has been so good for me to revisit all these channelings, these wonderful messages from my incredible support team. I hope you found them helpful as well.

My journal-writing, channelings and learnings have continued since this last journal entry in Mexico. My connection with Ramirah continues to change and evolve in major ways. But this is where I'd like to bring this part of the book to a close.

I'll wrap up this book with some key points. Frankly, these are things I'm still anchoring in as truth myself, still trying to embody. It's a process. Likely, it's a life-long process. I'm getting settled in for the long-haul.

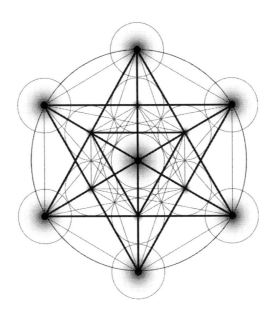

PART THREE:
ANCHOR IN THE TRUTH

When anyone follows her truth, she gives permission for everybody else to do the same.

- *The Book of Truth,* Channeled by Paul Selig

Gang, it's time to get real about a few things.

(I'm addressing you the reader, but I'm saying this to myself as well!)

- **This planet is changing on a massive scale, and we humans are changing along with it.**

   We've talked a lot about the ascension in this book. You can read more in my channeled book *Archangels, Aliens and Prophecies: The Cosmic Unveiling of a New Earth*, or research it online and through other books, articles and video sources. Now that you know about it, information will be plentiful. I'm guessing that we are maybe five to ten years away from this ascension becoming more common knowledge on a global scale. In the meantime, educate yourself and see what resonates. Maybe you, too, have a related calling and purpose here.

- **We are getting help from non-Earth entities with this transition.**

   Highly evolved beings from other realms, other planets, other dimensions are here to help and serve us as we make this major transition in vibrational frequency. Archangels like Archangel Metatron, Archangel Gabriel and Archangel Michael are actively involved with the ascension. Ascended Masters like Jesus, Saint Germain and John the Baptist are also working with us in their own ways. Extraterrestrials, aliens, non-terrestrial, highly evolved entities like Melchizedek are also massively involved with this ascension.

   All these beings have the capacity and the desire to connect with us telepathically, energetically, through dreams, and through other ways. This is FIRST CONTACT. These beings are helping the average person, people like me who HAD NO IDEA about any of this 18 months ago, to come to know the truth about our existence; the truth about all of existence and the multi-dimensionality of all creation. The truth that we are all one with source…the truth that separation and duality are illusions…the truth that Mother Earth and her people are ascending, and what that means for us. This is huge. This knowing allows us to dream of a new world that works much better than it does now. This is incredible and reason to celebrate. We are waking up to a new reality!

   Disclosure of alien life will be part of this ascension. We are being made aware of intelligent life outside this planet, coming now in small doses. Soon the proof will be massive and undeniable. The key here is to understand the benevolence of these entities. These entities who are making contact with the average person is a big part of the disclosure plan. Ask for a connection and be open to what comes your way. Ask for protection and ask to speak with only beings of love and light. Be specific with your questions.

- **Deal with your stuff.**

   The heightened energies coming to Earth right now as part of this ascension are amplifying EVERYTHING. It's no secret that things are nuts for a lot of people right now. Chaos and misery abound. If you have issues, problems, sadness, anxiety, roadblocks, shame, guilt, confusion, anger, grudges, regrets, etc., now is the time to work through those issues and resolve them. Three main points I'd like to make about this topic.

   First, we are being told time and time again to embody love right now. No fear, only love. We could spend a whole book talking about this concept. At the core, there is only fear or love. Fear is at the root of all "negative" emotions, whether that be self-hatred, feeling unworthy, feeling like a failure, holding anger, or blaming others. All of these are fear-based. If you harbor any feelings toward yourself or others that has its origin in fear, work to release that fear and move on. You must first love yourself before you can fully love others. This may include forgiveness, for yourself or others. It may include taking personal responsibility for yourself and your actions. Know that we are not separate from others but made from the same stuff. And we are all trying to do our best with what we've got in this lifetime.

I'd highly recommend Paul Selig's books for this; also, energy work such as Reiki; craniosacral work; body-based counseling like Hakomi; any self-care or alternative healing modalities that get to the core of the issues. Take time for yourself. Love yourself enough to take action to work through and resolve these issues. Do it now. We are being called to embody love for ourselves and then for others as our natural state of being. That love frequency acts as a tuning fork to help raise others' vibrations.

Second, it'll be very hard to raise your vibration and focus on love when you are miserable or experiencing pain and suffering of any level. The Melchizedek have explained to me that having a high vibration is the result of having alignment in your four-body system—mental, emotional, physical and spiritual. If something is out of alignment, you feel that in your energy frequency, your vibration.

Third, now is the time to learn your lessons for this lifetime. I fully believe that we all come to our different lifetimes with lessons we want to learn. Our soul brings us those experiences that will help us evolve, learn and grow. Your fear, pain, suffering, insecurities, issues, judgments, drama, etc., are here to teach you. Take the time to gain a broader perspective on your issues. Step back and see if there are recurring patterns that have become roadblocks for you. What do you need to learn to move on? My understanding is that our souls are looking to resolve old issues and learn lessons before the earth fully ascends. Our time is short to make this happen. Therefore, you may be feeling like there's more pressure or focus on your issues, and your life may feel frenetic. Problems may be slapping you in the face to be dealt with, finally. Know that the negative feelings that you hang onto have likely become a prison of your own making. Only you hold the key to that prison; only you have the ability to free yourself. You are in choice here.

All this being said, be gentle, loving and patient with yourself and your process.

- **Get quiet, every day.**

  You're going to have a much easier go of it if you take time to still your mind, quiet your energy and slow down. Get in touch with your energy frequency. Get in touch with your heart. We've lost that connection to our hearts, right? At least on a regular basis. I know I had. Get in touch with your breath. If we are always up in our head, formulating, thinking, scheming, worrying, writing to-do lists, our noses buried in our phones all day, we are not connected to our essence.

  We must reconnect with our authentic selves. Ponder our existence. Think beyond the every-day craziness of this life and connect with our higher selves. Connect to a higher source. Connect with our spirit guides. Connect with angels and highly evolved beings.

We all have free will, so you must ASK for that connection. Ask for help. Ask your questions. Journal often.

Don't get hung up on how to meditate if you are new to it. I know it can be daunting with all the breathing techniques and uncomfortable sitting positions. Make yourself comfortable and just start. The guided meditations by Steve Nobel on YouTube are lovely. But you don't need that. Find a quiet place on a couch or bed where you can have a bit of uninterrupted time and go from there.

- **We seem to have it all wrong.**

  I am asking my guides for help on articulating this point.

  For reasons beyond our normal understanding and out of our direct control, Earth was made to know itself through duality and separateness. (See the Urantia Book's description of the Lucifer Rebellion and *THE RETURN OF LIGHT: Revelations from The Creator God Horus* for more info on this.[9, 13]) The truth of the matter is that we are ALL manifestations of the Great Creator. I don't want to sound preachy or religious here—in fact just the opposite. Many organized religions declare that their religion is the "right" religion and other religions and ways of connecting to spirit are wrong. This continues to foster duality and separateness. We are all one, all made from the same stuff, and we are all connected in higher ways. To hurt another is to hurt ourselves. To judge another is to judge ourselves. We are constantly reflecting back to us that which we put out there.

  Think not with the mind on this point. It's not really something we can easily grasp with our mind. This is experiential and it comes from the heart. Our ego-mind is constantly in battle with our heart-mind, and this creates a ton of discord and strife in our lives. As we raise our consciousness, as we raise our vibration, we begin to see things in a new way. Our heart begins to take center stage. We begin to see our brother, mother, neighbor, friends, enemies in new ways. I do feel it is beneficial to first grasp these concepts intellectually, to have a basic mental understanding. From there, we open the door to new possibilities about life and how we relate to ourselves and each other until we experience it directly. Ideally, we are choosing to see everything in its divinity, as divinity in manifestation. This starts with seeing *ourselves* this way. Our outer realities change to reflect this new state of being.

  As we are born here on Earth, we forget that we are all one so that we may have this very unique experience; to learn our lessons and to evolve. This is the grand illusion. This is a playground for our souls. Remembering that we are all one is part of the game of evolution and growth.

IN CONCLUSION

Thank you so much for reading this book and for allowing me to share my journey with you. I'm feeling part terrified and part ecstatic to be putting these very personal experiences out there for the public; for my friends, acquaintances, past co-workers; for my family—immediate and extended. It is my sincere hope that this material helps you in some way.

I look forward to your feedback and questions, please reach out.

When I started talking to my spirit guide 18 months ago, I would have never guessed what was coming my way. What a roller coaster. I'm still hanging on for dear life. Some days I'm white-knuckled as I hang on tightly, and some days my arms are straight up in the air and I'm shrieking with delight. I am still experiencing quite a bit of anxiety around my transition.

With the publishing of this book, we'll see where my higher self and my guides take me.

I'm trying very hard to surrender to this process, to be open. To relax and go with the flow. To be fearless. This is still a bit of an uncomfortable place for me. I have to take this one day at a time and not over-plan anything. I'm trying to figure out the right balance between pushing and planning versus allowing and receiving in a more organic nature. No doubt, this is one of my life lessons.

I have an important mission, coupled with my twin flame.

I still don't know exactly how I'm going to be emancipating negative Reptilian energy from this plane. Another opportunity to relax into this process and surrender. I'll know what I need to know, when I need to know it. My amazing angelic and galactic support team has my back.

I also need to remind myself that I devised this plan before I incarnated.

I am fully in choice. This is why I'm here.

I believe that sharing our crazy stories and coming together collectively is extremely important. There is an urgency around what is happening. Experiences like mine are becoming more and more common. We are writing the playbook as we go…Get in, buckle up, enjoy the ride.

Many thanks and wishing you all the best in your personal journeys.

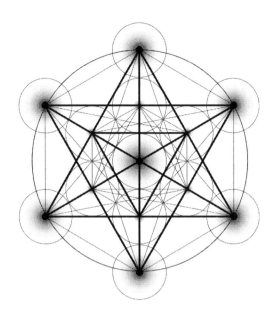

EXTRA: ARCHANGEL URIEL HEALING SEQUENCE

Way back in May of 2010, my sister said she'd gotten a message that Archangel Uriel wanted to connect with me. I had never consciously interacted with angels or even my spirit guide back then. But I was intrigued and willing to give it a try.

I was on a business trip at the time. I was staying at a hotel in Renton, Washington. I grabbed the hotel notepad and closed my eyes. I set my intention to connect with Archangel Uriel.

I just started writing down whatever came to me. What came was a hands-on healing sequence someone could perform with another person. I received visuals and words during this interaction.

I was doing quite a bit of Reiki at the time and was super excited about this. I tried the sequence with a couple close friends and sent it around to a few people. I felt that it was powerful. But at the time I didn't really know what to do with it.

I just found a hand-written note from July 2, 2012 that was tucked away with the original healing sequence. I don't remember this but I must have reached out to Archangel Uriel about this information two years after it came through. I wrote, "What am I to do with this sequence?"

The answer looks like another channeling from Archangel Uriel. He said,

"Really nothing. Just hold tight. The answers will be made abundantly clear to you very soon. No worries. You have so many gifts. This is but just one way to share your light and to serve the angels in this shift of consciousness."

Wow, this shift of consciousness! Sounds like he was referring to this ascension.

I guess now is the time to do something with this sequence—publish it with my book!

Please give it a try and let me know how it goes! Namaste.

Archangel Uriel Healing Sequence

Instructions for the person giving the healing sequence to another person:

- Person receiving the healing is standing
  - Go behind, left hand on left shoulder
  - Right hand above – call to universe
  - Scan with right hand, head down to below buttocks
    - Intention is to integrate the person's energy with the universal energy flow, which will move throughout the body
  - Move to feet – healer on your knees behind person, holding both ankles
    - Intention is grounding, strength, infallible security, connection to the universal energy on Earth and through the heavens
- Front – move to the front of the person receiving
  - Left hand behind heart on back, right hand on heart on front
  - Align your heart with theirs
  - Intention – open heart – feel love and support…
    1. Love for self
    2. Open to love = receiving
    3. Open to giving love
    4. Being love
  - Light-heartedness!
  - Feel a new way of relating to self and others
- Throat – full hand contact front and back of neck, under jaw
  - Intention is surrender, faith. There's no failing because you'll always be caught.

- Person receiving lays down
  - Left hand on their chest
  - Right hand above – again tune into that universal energy – "forces" a person to see, not deny, the help and healing
  - Scan head with the right hand, neck, shoulders, hara, triangle (hips and pelvis), inner thighs to knees
  - Go to feet
  - Raise both hands
  - Draw down (become) universal energy – "build" golden shoes (ball of energy) <u>under</u> each foot and around
- Integration
  - Person sits with legs crossed, hands on knees, finger/thumb together
  - Integrate for 5-10 minutes
  - Stand up – healer claps 3 x
  - Done.
- Repeat 1x per month for six months

ARTWORK & PHOTOGRAPHY DESCRIPTIONS

P. 30: Roykilva in watercolor

P. 38: Merkaba in watercolor

P. 67: Taken outside of my yurt, the day I arrived in Spa Buena Vista, March 2019

P. 69: The outside of my yurt; outdoor hot tub on the right

P. 72: Sunrise in Spa Buena Vista overlooking the Sea of Cortez, March 2019

P. 75: Me sitting in my hot-spring-fed outdoor hot tub at the yurt, March 2019

P. 78: Me walking on the beach with a friend in Spa Buena Vista, April 2019

P. 81: The main road through Spa Buena Vista; all the roads are sandy dirt, April 2019

P. 85: The stellar view out the front door of my yurt, March 2019

P. 89: Spa Buena Vista beach, April 2019

P. 91: Spa Buena Vista sunrise, March 2019

P. 94: Mountain bike and walking trail in the hills near Spa Buena Vista, April 2019

P. 97: Spa Buena Vista beach at dusk, March 2019

P. 103: Crystals and dragon-type being under the Earth's surface, watercolor

P. 108: Ramirah and me, watercolor

P. 113: Me typing in my journal in the yurt, April 2019

P. 120: Spa Buena Vista sunrise, July 2019

P. 124: Rocco on the beach in Spa Buena Vista, April 2019

P. 129: Roadside alter outside of Spa Buena Vista, April 2019

P. 133: Coral in the shape of a heart found at Punta Arena de la Ventana; Isla Cerralvo in the background, August 2019

P. 138: Sunset near Spa Buena Vista, April 2019

P. 143: Sunset in La Ribera, June 2019

P. 147: Me in front of Punta Arena de la Rivera Lighthouse, June 2019

P. 152: Spa Buena Vista sunrise, May 2019

P. 154: Rocco during one of our sunrise walks in Spa Buena Vista, July 2019

P. 159: Me at sunrise in Spa Buena Vista, June 2019

P. 163: Me fishing on a panga boat near Punta Arena de la Ventana and Bahia de Los Muertos, August 2019

P. 167: Colorful flags over a street in Todos Santos, August, 2019

P. 169: Sunset festivities on the Malecon in La Paz, August 2019

P. 171: Balandra Beach, La Paz, August 2019

P. 174: Me at Tortugueros Las Playitas Nature Preserve outside of Todos Santos, August 2019

P. 176: Playa Armenta, outside of Mulegé, August 2019

P. 178: Playa Armenta, outside of Mulegé, August 2019

P. 180: Me standing next to a giant Cordon cactus near Trinidad Canyon outside of Mulegé, August 2019

P. 182: Me on the beach at Playa Los Cocos (my favorite beach) outside of Mulegé; I stopped by here on my way to the airport in Loreto for one last set of photos, August 2019

P. 185: Using an un-popped corn kernel and a popped kernel to compare and contrast "Before Awakening" and "After Awakening", watercolor

SOURCES

1. Rueckert, C. *Living the Law of One 101: The Choice,* 2014.

2. Dronen, S. *Archangels, Aliens & Prophecies: The Cosmic Unveiling of a New Earth*, 2018.

3. Helen Schucman reference introduction. https://acim.org/acim/how-it-came-into-being/. Accessed Nov. 24, 2019.

4. Neale Donald Walsch background. https://en.wikipedia.org/wiki/Neale_Donald_Walsch. Accessed Nov. 24, 2019.

5. Walsch, N. D. *Conversations with God,* 1995.

6. Mackenzie, R. *Metatron – This is the Clarion Call: All You Need to Know*, 2011.

7. Carroll, L. Kryon channeling. http://www.kryon.com/CHAN2019/k_channel19_santafe.html. Accessed Mar. 21, 2019.

8. Cooper, D., Whild, T. *The Archangel Guide to Enlightenment and Mastery: Living in the Fifth Dimension,* 2016.

9. Gabriel, E., Kirschbaum, K. *THE RETURN OF LIGHT: Revelations from The Creator God Horus,* http://www.thenewearth.org/returnoflight.html, 2005.

10. Rueckert, C., McCarty, J. A., Elkins, D. *The Law of One: Book I - THE RA MATERIAL By Ra, An Humble Messenger of The Law of One,* 1984. www.llresearch.org

11. Ryan, C. O. *Ascension Manual: A Lightworker's Guide to Fifth Dimensional Living*, 2015.

12. Ryan, C. O. *Ascension Manual - Part Two: Creating a Fifth Dimensional Life*, 2016.

13. Urantia Foundation, *The Urantia Book*, www.urantiabook.org, accessed in 2019.

14. Selig, P. *The Book of Truth: The Mastery Trilogy: Book II,* 2017.

15. Foundation for Inner Peace, *A Course in Miracles (Second Edition)*, p. 560, 1992.

16. Goode, C. *Ascension & End Times Prophecy* - Corey Goode at Cosmic Waves - Part 1, online video, https://www.youtube.com/watch?v=rACn0u_zCD8. Accessed November 2019.